Fishing for Equilibrium

The Power of a Diary

By Kalila Volkov

For book ordering:
Kalilavolkov17@gmail.com
www.kalilavolkov.com

ISBN: 978-0-615-26317-5

Cover Illustration by Danya Volkov

Dedication

Thank you, dear witty and devoted husband, for your encouragement and your trust. You have a heart of gold. Thanks, darling girls, for loving and teaching me. You are my miracles. Mom, I am awed by how deeply you love me, and I adore you. Thank you for helping me to slow down. Dad, our being close now means the world to me. I can't thank you enough for all that you've given me. Brother dear, I marvel at your brains and accomplishments, and I'm thrilled that we hooked up as sibs this time around. You are an incredible composer, proofreader, inventor and uncle. Much appreciation goes to my high school English teacher, Mr. Provost, for getting me off to a good start, and to those tons of writers who shine and do it so well. I thank my extended family and friends for supporting me - I am proud to be connected to them all.

Author's Note: the italicized journal entries have been retained in their original format and have thus not come under the scrutiny of professional editing. Also note that movie and book titles have sometimes been underlined or placed in quotes to distinguish them from the journal entry italics.

CONTENTS

Introduction

Chapter 1   Hooked by the male mystique

Chapter 2   Just another awkward adolescence

Chapter 3   High school headaches and heartaches

Chapter 4   Falling for a handsome loser

Chapter 5   Words on paper made it safer

Chapter 6   Despair and disparagement

Chapter 7   Under the dorm roof

Chapter 8   Loving and leaving

Chapter 9   Wanderlust

Chapter 10   Quirky and working

Chapter 11   The fight to end the fight

Chapter 12   Boy chasing again

Chapter 13   Love is a many-splintered thing

Chapter 14   Plunder and split asunder

Chapter 15   Ultimately espoused

Chapter 16   The chemistry of sex

Chapter 17   The babyhood of Danya

Chapter 18   To hell and back

Chapter 19   Duo nuevo

Chapter 20   Giving it another go

Chapter 21   The arrival of a very boyish girl

Chapter 22   Travel and travail

Chapter 23   Then what

Chapter 24   Addendum:

*Holiday hyper

*Cursed with PMS and not sleeping

*The soft voice of reason

*Observations from middle age

*Something about death

*Random meanderings

*Faux poetry

*Final thoughts

As a teenager I was encouraged by this quote
and preserved it in my diary:

"*Keep a diary to see clearly – let none of the
nuances or small happenings escape even though
they might seem to mean nothing.*"
Jean-Paul Sartre

INTRODUCTION

Nothing terrible happened to me as a kid, but I was one of those girls who took everything personally (I still lean that way) and I needed to retreat, a lot. Now I don't know about you, but I'm willing to bet that if you grew up being a sensitive person like I did, you probably kept a diary. Or maybe you chose to write letters and leave notes rather than engage in uncomfortable conversations. If you too needed to pen your thoughts to others, or if you relied on "journal therapy" to feel better about yourself, then you are probably the best-suited reader for appreciating the personal account here. You would be more likely to relate to my need to write in order to make sense of the world. You might also be the type of person who enjoys reading published diaries because, like myself, you are curious about people; you find it intriguing to peer into others' lives through their written secrets, and know more about their hidden thoughts and honest feelings. So have at it, keeping in mind that most of the characters are shown in sketch form rather than portraits, as I mostly singled out that one person I know best—little ole' me. This memoir was written partly for family and friends, but I especially wanted to put it together for my fellow diary writers--past and present--who might find resonance in my story. However, this book may not be the type to make you want to leap from your chair and do a happy dance out of exhilaration because of its skillfully worked magic. My ending is joyful, certainly, but it's just that I'm a newbie who hasn't yet perfected the craft of those exceptional authors out there. It's reasonable to think that you may not clasp this book to your heart in ecstasy. And yet, sharing it with you is all I want to do.

A former babysitter gave me a journal for a gift long ago and she advised me *to fill the pages with problems and giggles. Save it, and twenty years from now it will bring back irreplaceable memories.* Following her advice I have kept journals to help me remember the details of my life that would have easily been forgotten otherwise.

I could never forget the fact that as a kid I ate Pop•Tarts™ for breakfast, and American cheese sandwiches with pretzel sticks for lunch nearly every day, but many special moments would definitely escape my memory if I did not have my writing as proof. Not only for that reason, I also wrote down my thoughts to understand myself better and to retreat from the world which often overwhelmed me.

I chose writing as both a way out and a way in---out of the mess that swirled around me as a growing girl, and within to that place where my soul spoke up. Looking for balance, I dropped the bait of self-inquisitiveness down to my inner core and fished around for answers. Writing helped me reel them in. Solutions sometimes darted behind a curtain of protection like jumpy trout being shadowed by their prey, but trying to hook some clues was a fun part of the process. The act of writing helped bits of the puzzle rise to the surface of my awareness as fish do at feeding time. When I envision myself as that young girl, I see her in a quiet place with a journal on her lap. She was a "heavy user"; she used the blank pages frequently to holler, question and celebrate. As an adult I haven't changed much. I haven't stopped being sensitive and I'm still not a big talker.

There was something about the way I was sitting today that made me feel like I was that girl at seventeen and not my age. For a flash my body felt quite young. My forty-nine years seemed to momentarily melt away, returning me to my vigorous but nervous youth. Was it because I was wearing ragged, faded jeans and sitting cross-legged in my classic writing position, filled with that familiar urgent desire to pour my heart out into my trusty notebook? Perhaps it was just that I was outside, alone with a journal to scratch in, snug against the warm wall of the house where I like to sunbathe. It was quiet, and I was content inside my private thoughts—that safe place where I lived so much while growing up. I continue to revel in the quietude of the introspective path, and I gravitate to libraries for the hush they provide. Libraries are marvelous hubs not only for their collections, but also for the way they can shelter us sensitive people— since fellow patrons are more focused on books, I find I'm not noticed and judged as much as when I'm outside in the bigger world, trying to keep a safe space around me among the hustle and bustle. With such a thin skin, I have always been intimidated by the judgments of other people. Journeying back through my memories reveals why I clung to the comfort of writing as a way of processing input, handling others' opinions, and retreating from distress. Keeping a diary has also been a tool for me for holding open the space in my head that sees magnificence and insists on praising it.

My girls probably won't believe this is their mom's story.

Interspersing stories and reflection with diary entries from the sixties and beyond, I share my journaling partly as a peek back into the world when postage stamps were eight cents and there were no CDs, HDs, camera phones or the web. Risking embarrassment I give you stories of teenage heartbreak, historical tragedies, spiritual upheaval, romantic struggles and other wholesome goodies. I also present my little stories out of a sincere need to a) offer them as testament to how wacky and wonderful our earthly time is, b) document them simply for preservation and c) display them as evidence that journaling can provide sanctuary. I also give you poems because they are my favorite things to write. They are my attempt to glorify nature and express my gratitude for the world's abundant beauty.

Join me in these pages as I journey around the Candyland™ board of life, landing not only in the swamps of troubled emotions, but also on the peaks of the sweetest tenderness. Observe how wickedly clever babies can be. Witness how you too can give your life to PMS. Just for fun I include some sex, politics and angels. These pages will no doubt prove I am bonkers despite my having had several counseling sessions; but there's a good chance you will derive some entertainment from them.

All I know is that writing and journal-keeping are what ground me to this illusory earth, and I heartily recommend the discovery of one's soul through this process. It's inexpensive therapy! Join this troop of fellow "journalinguists" and give your inner voice a place to cry and fly free. (Some famous diarists include Louisa May Alcott, Ralph W. Emerson, Anne M. Lindbergh, Harry S. Truman, and Anne Frank, of course.) Elaine Aron said it beautifully in her book *The Highly Sensitive*

Person: a person who writes down their moods, musings and miracles will become part of the long tradition of journal-keepers.

◆◆◆◆◆◆◆

Please note that up until the age of twenty-one my name was Kelly. I changed my name when I was a hippie, but if possible I would have changed it when I was eight: I hated the taunting I received at the neighborhood bus stop when I had to hear "Kelly, Kelly, belly full of jelly." I've been told that Kalila (ka-LEE-la) means "flute" in Hawaiian and "friend of God" in Lebanese.

POETRY SNACK

I glanced down at just the right moment to see your darling, cheerful face – magenta, five petals, tiny white dot in the center. You fascinate me with your cosmic, geometric design, your mandala shape.

You were itty-bitty but packed with the power to brighten this humble hiker's path. Everywhere else, yellow dominated the fields, mostly suncups and wallflowers.

If the trail hadn't been so rocky (I love it that way), I would not have been watching my steps and spied you.

In that instant I became part of the trinity of you, me, and my dog trotting merrily ahead of me. Then, we were all so free.

HOOKED BY THE MALE MYSTIQUE

I don't have a clue why I was so enchanted by the opposite sex at a fairly young age, and it's a wonder I didn't end up being a tramp. (Oh but wait, I did, briefly.) At ten, quite a few decades back to 1969, boys were one of THE main things on my mind. I was a romantic early on. There was something about the beauty of boys that fixated me. I viewed them with an artistic perspective, like they were lovely portraits or sculpture. Was it because I was kissed on the swings in kindergarten even though I had beaver teeth? I hadn't even watched that many chick flicks as a kid – only a few Doris Day films and a couple of Hepburns. (Was I already looking outside of myself for completion?) The Beatles were okay, but I adored Micky and Davy from The Monkees, along with other young actors of the day. If I could have eaten what I bought in teen idol magazines those days, I would be off the scale. While snacking on energy fad-food known as Space Food Sticks, I feasted on photos of my favorite cute smiling heads. Sometimes my fantasies of meeting stars would consume my lusty thoughts, and I would *act plum cracked over Vincent Van Patten, David Cassidy, Bobby Sherman... I didn't mind living off dreams.* I pictured meeting them and wooing them with my radiance. Yet when my parents offered to take me on a movie studio tour in L.A. when our family was on vacation, I feared having an actual encounter with a hunk and was too paranoid to go. I was an insufferably insecure girl who spent inordinate amounts of time in imaginative fantasies. My shyness may have resulted from our having moved many times. My dad worked in aerospace so we bounced around from Los Angeles, to Seattle, to the Hartford area, to Houston and then back to Connecticut. (We even lived in a motel for a while, but that's another story.) I also reasoned that with my braces, plain features, ski slope nose and acute timidity, I didn't have much to offer boys in real life.

Should a coveted teen actor happen to appear on TV, *I would smile a super smile like they were going out of style. The excitement would be too much for me. Like in school today. I was bored to hell, even though hell isn't boring, so I decided to daydream about my favorite guys. When I look back on this time of my youth, I'll remember this period as a happy one. Mom thinks I'm boy crazy, but she's just plain crazy...*

In fact, I was so nutso that I played a little game that allowed me a glimpse into a pretend future to see if I might end up with a certain boy. It was called FRIENDSHIP COURTSHIP MARRIAGE LOVE HATE. I wrote my name and the "candidate's" name on a piece of paper. I then crossed out all of the same letters that appeared in my name that also appeared in his name. Lastly, I counted off the remaining letters in each name and recited "Friendship Courtship Marriage Love Hate;" one of these choices became my final verdict. If I didn't like the result, I tried using full names complete with a middle name to get a better answer. It was divination at its finest! (My vanity forces me to explain that I did not make this game up myself, as another elementary school girl taught it to me.)

Since I certainly wasn't about to claim anyone famous for myself, I became more realistic. I was ready to focus on the more attainable of the boy species and swoon over a local guy. I quietly loved Peter from fourth grade all the way through eighth. He had long, neat brown hair and, although his nose was not large, his brown eyes were. I admired everything about him, from his school clothes to the way he drew on his book covers. We even had something in common: we both liked the band Chicago! It made me flush to watch him play baseball, and I would peer at him from behind the chain link fence at the park, cherishing the perfection that was his small body as he ran around the bases in his cute white uniform. When he got on the fifth grade football team, I made my move to be close to him and tried out for cheerleader. My flexibility and coordination were only average, and while I could never achieve a proper cartwheel or walkover, the coach took me anyway. Peter never noticed how passionately I cheered for him on the sidelines, and of course I never spoke to him. In school when I walked past him in the halls, I couldn't even look him in the eyes without blushing. Despite my attraction to him, I knew *he wouldn't settle for girls like me. The in-betweens.* I figured, who would notice, much less like, such a quiet girl who was neither a "real" cheerleader nor a trendy "freak"?

Happier days existed in the summertime when I was free of the stresses of school and the mire of having a crush. I had a friend named Bini whose family owned a second home on Cape Cod and I got to stay for a week. Once I recovered from homesickness, I treasured our daily excursions to the beach, despite the ugliness of some of the sea creatures cast about from the tide. To my chagrin, I discovered the unattractive horseshoe crab with its huge shell that looked like a Darth Vader™ helmet on the sand. Its hideous form shattered the beauty of the beach and I was afraid of the crabs chasing me. Bini and I had a custom of naming the different lucky rocks we collected (those with cool stripes) and lining them up on a paper towel on her bureau. I loved the dock with the dressing rooms, *where there was the usual clutter of sandy towels, buoys, shells and smelly bathing suits, and where there were the signatures of all the kids each year on the walls.* I loved riding our bikes down to the post office on the corner and then riding back, taking not the shortcut but the long bumpy way, and then finishing our jaunt by riding around the porches on the house and down the stairs. In those innocent, carefree moments we tasted the joy of childhood.

A favorite game Bini and I played was a pretend version of hypnotism. We took turns being the hypnotist, putting the other in a "spell" and directing her to do (normal, not weird) things upon command. Whoever was under fake hypnosis would close her eyes, act as if in a trance and move about like a puppet. Bini and I wanted so much for our magic to work and for our dramatic performances to seem convincing that we played this game numerous times when we were together. Our special evening activity was playing "Murder in the Dark" with Bini's pack of siblings. I liked the challenge of remembering where the coffee table and grandfather clock were positioned in the living room when I had my eyes closed, desperately trying to avoid bumping into the furniture and the kid who was playing the murderer.

Another challenge I faced that vacation was trying not to freak

3

out while Bini learned to sail as I kept her company on the small boat. I didn't have great sea legs, and even though she seemed confident about her abilities, I was holding on with a death grip. We weren't sailing solo for long when the boat capsized. I remember feeling frantic that I would be trapped, unable to swim out from underneath the boat. The water was freezing and the shock of suddenly being dumped into it made it feel a lot colder. Our rescue wasn't immediate and I feared being touched by a slimy, creepy sea animal. And even though I loved salt, I'd gulped in way too much seawater. Once I had forgiven her for our mishap, Bini and I sealed our relationship by becoming blood sisters. It took us several days of mental preparation to build up the nerve to extract blood from our bodies. We waited until one of us had a cut and then watched while the other found a scab to poke, and blended our blood in a ritual that, to us, was of cosmic proportions.

The summer I was thirteen, my family headed south from Connecticut to visit relatives in Louisiana. I liked my older cousin Dave but fell in love with Stephen who was twelve. I found him sweet and irresistible and felt guilty about it. He attracted me with his fine manners and Southern hospitality and I wished we weren't related. Since I had to keep my fondness for him undercover, I acted like a detective who kept track of Stephen's interests. When he liked something I didn't, I committed it to memory. Then I hoped to impress him in subsequent conversations by referring to those tidbits I had learned about him to build up our rapport. At our uncle's ranch we chatted and joked while leaning over the barn gates, and I adored his cool casual way of moving. I cherished his style.

There was a particularly funny incident: Steve had taken his jeans to his mom for a zipper repair. His mom asked for thread by saying, "There's a hole in the fly and his thing's coming out." (She meant his jean flap and not **his** actual thing.)

The grocery store names I saw in Louisiana were a crackup: The Wag-a-Bag™, The Pac-A-Sac™, and The Piggly Wiggly™. My boozer aunt drove the family around town while swigging bourbon out of a flask. I enjoyed viewing brick houses with wrought-iron gates, pineapple growing in front yards and moss hanging bountifully on the trees. Visiting more relatives on a lake nearby, we northerners got to experience the bayou with its levees, houseboats, pontoons and motorboat rides. One night while riding back from the lake (the day that I nearly crashed the motorboat I was driving), my brother and our cousins and I were sitting in the open truck bed enjoying the bouncy ride. Because I was under love's spell at the time, the scene had a particularly magical charm to it -- every detail was sweet and fresh. It was as if rhapsodic notes from an orchestra were swelling in the background and making me even more love struck. I took in everything with pleasure, *the fishing poles that rattled in their buckets, the sugary air that smelled of fresh-cut hay, and the catfish that flipped weakly in the cooler.* I stole many glances at the boy I fancied, watching his hair blowing around in the wind. The dark road ahead appeared endless, birds sang out in the rolling fields, and those moments were forever imprinted on my tender heart.

It was refreshing to be around these Southern boys who were polite, in contrast to my younger brother Scott who endlessly annoyed me. Scott irritated us by calling the boys dumb names like "Crinkle-Tit" and "Snickle." If they said to him, "You're a jerk," he'd reply, "So is your face." He also had an obnoxious habit of saying to me, "Look at them knockers," or, "Let me give them a squeeze." Scott was also infamous at age five--at which time we called him Scooter--for ramming a pencil into my kneecap when I didn't feel like writing out his Christmas list to Santa. (Now that I am older, I am grateful that I recorded these events and remarks, rather than losing them to the ethers. So much would have been buried if I hadn't. Jot it down, people, the good and the bad! After all, your family might need a historian.)

However, Scott and I didn't fight and provoke each other on the regular car trips in the summer to the Connecticut shore; we were either too sleepy or too excited to argue. We packed up with our mom and left early; the tedious two-hour drive each way was tolerable since we would spend the rest of the day by the ocean. Traffic typically slowed once we left the freeway and inched our way through the small towns close to the beach. Approaching our destination, we felt our spirits lift as we caught site of the expansive blue view of the Atlantic that signaled freedom, relaxation, warmth and play. Catching that first big whiff of salty air and Coppertone™ was always a delight, but arriving at the ocean brought irritation as well as relief. Lugging our beach gear a long way from the packed parking lot to the crowded sand made us grouchy. Scott usually complained, our mom then chided him and I carried scratchy, fraying beach chairs that always banged into my legs.

I liked the ritual of laying out our old camping blanket once we'd scouted a decent spot. Because of the intense heat that penetrated the nice sea breeze, I had to take a dip quite often to keep my blood from boiling. Even though I had a thin shapely figure, I did not relish going in and out of the water for fear of people staring at my curves. I held off going into the water for as long as I could.

Lunches from the Coleman™ camp cooler were yummy. It didn't matter to me that the cheese sandwiches were soggy since food tasted better outside. Everything got sandy of course, whether it was from the wind or from the young kids who ran by, kicking sand up onto the blanket and into our eyes and mouths. Scott and I could never stand the heat to wait a full hour after eating to enter the water.

I have fond memories of going to Misquammicut Beach those hot July days regardless of the near-death experiences I had on different visits there. As it happened, the drop-off was close to shore, so my feet didn't touch bottom if I wanted to ride the better waves breaking farther out. I always wanted to position myself where I could float or bob up and down on the waves just before they crashed – where they would give me a gentle lift, just prior to their big surge. The trouble was, I wasn't a great judge of the timing or power of the waves. They often trapped me mercilessly, flipping me several times and dashing me into the rocky floor, often rendering me clueless as to which way was up. These were the times I relied on some inner plea to hold on for just a few more seconds, having to trust that I would survive the calamity even when I was convinced I had no more air left. Having nearly drowned left me quite exhausted, and I emerged from the sea with my hair clumped around my bewildered face, my bikini dripping and askew, and my feet stinging with cuts from the rocks. I then flopped my drained, achy body onto the (ugh) sandy blanket and counted my lucky stars for having survived.

Once I felt restored, I found it soothing to listen to all of the sounds around me: the roar of the water, squeals of kids getting splashed, parents yelling, babies crying, umbrellas flapping, soda cans being popped open, and American Top 40™ songs playing from various transistors. I focused on the way my skin felt when the water evaporated that made it feel crusty and tight, only to tighten even more as it burned. The sun seemed to sear into my flesh.

You and others might criticize my enjoyment of peeling and being peeled; my family thought it was disgusting and encouraged me to stop it. I carried on gleefully in private, wondering if I had reptiles in my ancestry because I loved peeling so much. It was equally as pleasurable for me to nip at and carefully pull off the flaky pieces of skin from my own body, as it was to do so from someone else's. I particularly liked peeling the larger "sheets" from the back and relished the wispy sound that peeling made, the tissuey quiet noise heard as flesh separated from itself. Viewing the peeling process later in life, I saw that in the crispy instant when the old detached from the new, there was a subtle reminder of the bigger picture---a fragment of symbology, showing that every little tear away from our illusionary separate body could bring a tiny rebirth. I felt lighter after peeling because of its resulting underlay of perfect skin freshness.

Odd behaviors aside, those beach days of my youth stood out as flags to honor the school-free months, back when summer school was only for the luckless underachievers. In current times good students go to summer school to stay ahead and keep up with the competition. Knowing firsthand the feeling of having an unencumbered summer that seemed to stretch into forever, I have felt remorse for kids today who join in the rat race so early.

It was during one of those glorious relaxed summers when my family vacationed at a church camp in southern Maine that, at fourteen, I took my interest in boys one step further. I was unsure if I had been smitten with Andy because of his goofy nature, his charming Southern drawl or because of his wickedly curly hair. Once we had hooked up, we joined three other couples that hung out in a cabin after dinner and learned how to make out. Thankfully no one made any disgusting slurpy sounds and we were able to blissfully ignore the mosquitoes. Since Andy was a year younger I felt funny kissing him, but as he said, "Age is not important when love is involved." Kissing while being congested, Andy had to take a break and claimed, "My ears can't breathe that long."

One morning I ate breakfast with Lydia who was a member of the kissing club. Lydia burned her tongue on her coffee and said, "Oh, it won't be any good tonight!" Her mother just about died.

Not having known that Andy was a fan of W.C. Fields and frequently used Mr. Field's material, I thought it was funny when he whistled at some girls walking a dog and said, "I'm whistling at the dog."

Back home from that sexy summer, I compared notes with a friend. I felt happy that Libby too had become experienced in French-kissing, and we wondered about why we felt sick to our stomachs afterward. I also felt sick from missing Andy and obsessed about our short-lived connection. I couldn't keep from watching our home movies over and over, where I would see my gang of friends walking from the campground up to the cafeteria—all in a line, bumping shoulders, and teasing each other recklessly. Watching those reels, I could squint and see Andy's darling grin just one more time.

JUST ANOTHER AWKWARD ADOLESCENCE

Peer pressure was intense for me at age fourteen. My girlfriend really wanted to start smoking cigarettes because everyone was doing it. I wrote, *I've made it so far and I don't feel square at all. Kids nowadays think that you're only tough and cool if you smoke something and/or go to 4th base. Doesn't anyone dig a person's personality and true self?* After the movies one night, back when they cost only $1.50, young kids were smoking in a crowd and my friend really wanted a cig. I didn't feel compelled to try smoking because I had frizzed my hair and its freaky bushiness gave me a self-assured satisfaction. I thought I was Hip Kid Number One, cool like Janis Joplin, and didn't need a cigarette in my hand to assert my coolness. I discovered that braiding my hair was relaxing, and that if I braided wet hair and slept on it, the next day it would have a good kink to it. Was I ever a kinky chick! By making many smaller braids rather than five bigger hunks, my hair came out wild! My mom sacrificed the time to do the braiding and I got to take the tightly woven braids out, carefully undoing them before getting on the school bus in the morning. Mom confirmed the Janis Joplin resemblance and I beamed to be presenting a bolder, more rebellious side to myself. A part of me liked the attention I got, looking hipper than usual. My persona temporarily merged into the freak clique and I enjoyed the brief notoriety that came with a more radical image. Otherwise, my status among my peers was undefined. The high school in Simsbury (it rhymes with berry, not furry) sported plenty of cheer-leaders and jocks as well as "hoods" and early "goth" girls. You re-member, I belonged neither to the prissy/popular crowd nor the rowdy/ tough kids. I felt like a misfit and was self-conscious around other kids of any clique. *It's like there are classes within the teenage population. It's hard to get into certain "groups of friends" if one friend doesn't approve. Walking down the halls in school, I feel everyone is staring or thinking I'm stuck-up. Plus, what I'm going to wear is always a problem. I'm a worrywart, but of course, I'm a girl.* It was this timid side to me that loved hiding under all of the frizzy hair.

For awhile, simple things eased the stress of being a teen, like kinking my hair or getting my ears pierced; it made me feel really grown up. *I jet around thinking I'm the toughest kid there ever was. I have discovered that many things can turn me on, so that I can rely on them and not on drugs. Windy days, thunder storms, movie stars, adventure. If I stay at the rate I'm going, I may MAKE IT!* There seemed to be an ongoing pressure for me to be different from who I was: to try drugs and be cool, to get more friends, or find other ways to fit in better. But back then I thought I wouldn't succumb to the temptation to experiment with drugs. Writing in my journal helped me sort out my frustrations with school, friends, parents and myself. *Ah hello dear journal, all day I've been excited about spending some time with you.* I used my journal as an outlet for my boy obsessions, my worries and my dreams. Keeping a diary also helped me as a grown woman retrace those priceless episodes and activities from childhood that I treasured, evidenced in the following memories: hearing a trickling sound that came from a nearby desk in school and then realizing a classmate was peeing in his pants (first grade); pulling erasers out of pencils, drawing faces on them and carrying them around each day (second grade); standing in line after recess asking those around me, "What does fuck mean?" and observing their eerie silence (third grade); coloring geography maps and labeling one hundred and twenty-five things on them which took forever (sixth grade); and lastly, remembering that fateful science class when we studied what poop was made of (eighth grade).

Weather played a special role in the life of us school kids living in New England. I belonged to that group of peers that delighted in having school cancelled for whatever reason, and I remember some years when school was closed a couple of times in winter. What a blissful feeling it was when Mom buzzed over the intercom (it was so cool and unusual to have such a thing) not to wake me up, but rather to inform me that school was called off for the day. Not only did we have those occasional school closings (never often enough) due to blizzards or ice storms, we also got to go home for other reasons. We were sent home because of "January thaw" when the temperature went from 10 to 50 degrees quite rapidly, making it terribly foggy and creating hazardous driving conditions. Then near the end of school, one year the heat reached 100 degrees in the shade by 9:00 in the morning. Many classes were allowed to sit out in the halls where it was cooler and then students were let out at noon.

Things were heating up for me at home too. Fights between my parents and my brother were common and my heart ached from the frequent yelling and swearing matches. The Happy Hour cocktails, which our parents used to obtain happiness and to discuss solutions, didn't soothe the tension. I slipped away as much as possible and hid my pain by writing. Grief spilled out too, like when I lost a schoolmate in a terrible accident. A girl who recently started driving had friends in her car when an electrical problem sparked an engine fire. The passengers weren't wearing their seat belts and were able to escape, but the girl was trapped by her belt and burned to death.

◆ ◆ ◆ ◆ ◆ ◆ ◆ ◆

At fifteen, life had its many awkward, challenging moments. For starters, there was my awful acne. Top that off with braces, chronic canker sores and the frizzy hair. Then came prominent boobs and one hard contact lens that gave my right eye terrible pain due to dust, wind and smoke. (Oddly enough I wore only one contact.) This age brought with it friendship problems, more family conflicts and the need to keep retreating inside myself. Writing in my diary had always been a pleasant hobby but now it was a panacea. It was my main coping mechanism. I didn't like exposing much expression on my face—it made me feel too vulnerable, so I wrote my feelings down instead.

Often Mom asked, "What are you going to do now, Kelly?"

"I'm gonna write in my diary."

I love to write and think every kid should have a diary, and write in it as much as they can. If not, so many good moments will pass them by, and when they are older, they'll forget most of them, the bad ones too. My life is revealed in you, diary -- the music of my mind always playing, the joy of my days always within me. I am reaching, searching, and loving, and wasting my bloody time writing in you! But nah, I have grown up with you. Writing relieves a lot of strife, puts me into a good mood, and/or eases my mind...

Watching the sky served to settle my nerves and ease my mind too. It was my way of taking a writing break, looking up and out, both to jump back into the outer world, and to hunt for the words I needed to express. I have been a big fan of the sky and its constant metamorphoses---its dabs of paint swirls, its alternate gifts of serene sunny-ness and foreboding shroud---and only recently have I understood my affinity for it. I admire how the sky feels so free to reveal its "emotions." It doesn't second-guess itself or question what colors to present, what cloud shapes to present, or how much precipitation it creates. While becoming a young adult, I, on the other hand, costumed myself with falsity---hiding my shadows away, covering the gloom with smiles and damming up the floods of tears. Storms alarmed me with their urgent intensity, but the low-wattage inner tempests that have long-since passed could have been powerful sources of current for me. I chose not to tap into them. I didn't want to burn.

One time when our family went out for dinner at a restaurant, I tried to avoid the scorch from the fight my parents were having with Scott. They really told him off. Perhaps he was showing bad manners or complaining about the menu. I just sat there, numbly reading over and over the words "unsweetened grapefruit drink" to keep from getting involved or feeling hugely upset. I felt so embarrassed that I wanted to make an incision in the family and slice my life away from them. I could have demanded, "Will you guys knock it off?" but was too reticent to delve into the conflict.

Writing was a lifesaver once we started family counseling. When Scott heard we had to visit a psychiatrist he put his favorite blanket over his head. Unfortunately we went only twice. I had my journal to escape into, but Scott used more physical means to react to arguments. After Scott and Dad had a big fight, I heard Scott push his bed against the door. Then, Dad stood at the door and bawled Scott out with hurtful words and curses. I wrote, *Seems to me that Scott is having an awful time growing up.*

My dad and I would clash too. We got into trouble when he tried helping me with my math homework. I was sometimes slow in picking up a concept, he did not possess a ton of patience, and it seemed we had a frequent pattern of miscommunicating. My typical reaction was to get flustered and feel intimidated. When he became mad, he carped and cussed and I responded demurely. If he'd had a drink, he became even more intense, so I developed a mistrust of him and his moods. Booze meant tension. It meant Dad could fly off the handle. Alcohol seemed to have enormous power to transform a person into a monster that constantly changed shape. Dad didn't often swear at me, but he often did because of me. Most of the time the swear words were hurled towards Scott. As soon as I heard the tone of Dad's voice escalate, I felt a rise in body heat and blood pressure and had wet armpits. If I overheard an altercation going on elsewhere in our house, it usually helped if I kept quiet and stayed out of the way. I didn't like being physically near the harsh words and they stung even when they weren't directed at me. I perfected the art of placating and thus developed a habitual reaction of saying, "I'm sorry." Dad would tell me to stop defending myself but would then turn around and advise me to stand up for my rights. The mixed messages confused me. The good news was that he also dished out encouragement and praise. We were talking about someone one day and, because I had kept an open mind about the situation, Dad remarked, "Kelly, you always give people the benefit of the doubt."

"Wow, thanks." My eyes lit up. I was so happy he noticed.

Regardless of how bleak our family relationships seemed some days, I would later understand that my parents did the best they could. I believe that people choose their parents and I truly value the lessons mine taught me. The wisdom now provided by being a parent myself has allowed me a much greater appreciation of their childrearing trials and the sacrifices they made. It is a saving grace, and an amazing place to come to, when we children grow up to see our parents on an adult-to-adult level. The relationships I have with mine have been mollified and modified over time that it's as if we are all different people, yet I know that love and forgiveness simply forged a new connection of inexorable strength.

Gifts galore have spilled into my life from my parents' hands like a piñata's booty. I have long been on the receiving end of my dad's generosity, but he also is altruistic and supports friends, family members and his community. I am particularly indebted to him for encouraging me to write and sing. How wonderful that we survived my adolescence together and that our communications are now friction-free! I honor Dad for handing down his love of jazz, good words and hikes in the woods. He blows me away by being so fit in his seventies that he blazes past me when we climb up the hills behind my house. Being the Zodiac sign of Cancer, my mom's gifts are plentiful, for she takes her role seriously and overflows with caring. Listing the pleasures we have shared and the many things she's taught me would run off the page, but I certainly would not be doing her justice if I didn't mention a few of them. For one thing, she painstakingly blew Easter eggs by hand and decorated them to look like our family and the cat. For another, when I was a kid she often spoiled me and left surprises on my bed like a new book, jewelry or clothes. Mom, being the sophisticated woman from the South that she is, instructed me in the importance of good manners, buying goods of high quality (especially shoes) and taking the time to do things well. She also happens to be one of the most considerate people I know. At times I would think that the phrase "Yes, Mother" could be interpreted as "Yes, Smother," but in most respects I regard her as a mega godsend, a true embodiment of deep motherly love. She constantly teaches me how powerful it is to be a mother and I know how lucky I am to be close with her. I will forever respect her for being a great listener and witty conversationalist, teaching me responsibility, and for having an amazing memory useful for preserving the stories of her childhood and mine. Even though it's not a pleasant remembrance for her, I love when she tells the story about the rooster that attacked her feet when she was walking home from school in second grade.

As an adult I felt badly that as a typical teenager I was so critical of my parents. I judged everything they did and said. (Now it's my turn for payback: my kids seem pretty critical of me, especially when I act silly. It's karma in action!) I found fault in everything from Dad's morning coffee breath down to the way Mom nitpicked about little things. Dad would inadvertently contribute to my disrespect of him by coming to lunch baring a sweaty hairy chest and no shirt (needing to finish mowing the lawn after eating). Somehow, though, camping trips were nearly always the perfect venue for family bonding, and our personalities became more congenial to one another as we fused in harmony with the peacefulness of being out in the woods. My esteem for Dad shot up when we went camping because he told exciting ghost stories, cleverly showed off his many Boy Scout leader skills, and sparked in me a mighty reverence for trees. On one legendary camping trip our family got stuck in a terrible storm, and poor Mom, the martyr, stood all night in the downpour, holding up our tent roof so that it wouldn't collapse on us. Thanks, Mom, for that sacrifice and for all the other times that we didn't notice.

HIGH SCHOOL HEADACHES
AND HEARTACHES

My journals became more intense and extensive as high school rolled on. Life was indeed more complicated. I had now entered a period of drug experimentation, rock and roll concerts, strong emotions and the desire for a steady boyfriend. I reported, *I'm worrying because school gets so complex. Something happening every day: work, basketball, things to remember, assignments to finish, long-term reports to start on, piano practice, etc. I think I've got the teenage blues. It's boredom, inactivity, and restlessness in one! I went for a walk and it didn't help. I played the piano but it didn't help. I called friends and no one was around. Maybe I oughta call HotLine to talk. I think I've been around Mom and Dad for too long.*

There seemed to be many milestones and teenager tests those days. I survived one nerve-racking high school moment when I asked a guy I liked but didn't know well to my sixteenth birthday party. Bill was a tall, mysterious basketball player. After I left his homeroom in school I was pale from the shock. When Bill said he could come to my party *I felt like screaming with delight and passing out and stuff!* The thought of having Bill at my party ended up being better than the actual thing. I felt nervous around him and we didn't have conversations that clicked well. When my party pals and I strolled over to the golf course across the street that night, I didn't know how to hook his attention. While everyone was running around and acting silly, the chance of my engaging Bill became even more scattered. He left earlier than my closer friends had, but at least I had given him a chance. I was upset we hadn't hit it off. A desperate part of me had wanted to join the group of my friends who got to hold hands on the golf course with a boy they liked.

Sleepover parties were just as popular then as they still are today. For no particular reason I can recall, I had a girl party one

Saturday night. In anticipation of the event I wrote, *We'll probably do charades, eat, watch the late shows, eat, have a séance, and eat... It turns out we called four boys, played lots of albums and at 3:30 went to bed!*

Since I was not an outgoing person, I had a small circle of friends. Alison was my best buddy, and she spent time with me when she wasn't hanging out with a boyfriend or riding her horse Sprite. She had brown hair down to her butt, big blue eyes and cheeks that regularly flushed bright pink. She blew her nose a lot. Loudly. I loved the way she would swing her long hair around to move it out of her way, looking a bit like Sprite when he shook his mane. Being goofy, Al and I liked to transform ourselves into grunting apes. We never sneaked out of the house or anything radical like that. Instead, one of our favorite activities was riding bikes at night, even as late as 11:00 pm. I would sing Allman Brothers to drown out Al's off-key Led Zeppelin. Living in the country we could zip around dark quiet neighborhoods and never worry about cars. At bedtime, we gossiped, fantasized, and intimately spilled our guts while gazing at the Gregg Allman poster on her ceiling. She was my sounding board. She showed me I was okay when I wasn't so sure. Al was also fun because of her bubbly personality and she kept me easily amused. Once when my dad took us out to dinner, she embarrassed herself a few times by accidentally spitting on him, dropping salad in her lap, and laughing with wine in her mouth (we were old enough).

Al had a party once where there was a ratio of four girls to ten guys. *It was a total cosmic riot because a few guys got on this hang-a-moon kick.* We eventually played Spin the (Ketchup) Bottle. A kid named Rich sat outside the circle and no one invited him in. (All the girls thought he looked like a monkey. I hoped he was either gay or at least unscarred by this incident.) I kissed six guys. All the girls later took turns giving a report on each partner. Jeff had kissed me twice – because he wanted to, or had I flubbed the first one?

I really liked Jeff, Al's former boyfriend. He had the greatest smile and looked like a California surfer. I think my crush started when he threw coffeecake at me at school and it went down the front of my shirt. Even though Al had a new honey, it felt strange for me to be close with Jeff. Despite his huge appeal, it seemed too bizarre to date my best buddy's last sweetheart. We were never a couple but had shared a few intimate times, and I documented, *At a concert Jeff put his arm around my waist and OOOOOH sheesh I couldn't believe it! Plus, we had a great conversation – we spoke like old friends, not hung up about what to say or about what's been said. Then he asked, "Kelly, wanna kiss?" I freaked out! He put a Hershey's™ into my hand.* The flirting was enjoyable but opening fully to Jeff made me tense. He was much too cute, his teeth were too white and I was simply too nervous. I wonder, had I been afraid that he would compare me with Al and find me lacking? Did I think he was too perfect for me, or that he was just teasing me? It felt like the ghost of his relationship with Alison was bumping around between us. Sadly, I couldn't allow him to get into my sequestered heart. (I would go on to involve myself in many more romantic quandaries.)

Maybe it got to the point that I was "hard up" when I agreed to go out with Jimmy, the greasy long-haired dude who had a horse named Lucky and who got to drive his family's yellow Cadillac. He was younger (again?) but more experienced. One afternoon we met in his family's barn, and I noted that we were "busy" for quite some time; we listened to four albums, some more than once. Even though Jimmy and I went out for just a short time, it was still a big deal for me to suddenly have a boyfriend. I felt like I fit into a new group and felt more secure. Increasingly I was gaining confidence and not blending into the crowd all the time. At home, however, I persisted in being rebellious yet shy. Any time my parents had someone over in the living room, I would try to sneak upstairs; from the hallway I took off my shoes and crept up the stairs to my room, or maybe even climbed over the banister without making a sound. Being stealthy was a good challenge to pull off, as I abhorred being asked to play the piano for company. I detested the attention, especially from people who were drinking. Their annoying guffaws and their loud volume of conversation disturbed my peace. If I happened to get caught by their gaze, I put on an act of niceness and tried to quickly zip out of the room.

(Once I was in the safety of my bedroom, I did enjoy listening to the sound of my dad's albums rising upstairs – those by Sergio Mendes, Horace Silver, Herb Alpert and other cool jazz cats. Little did I know Dad was giving me a free jazz appreciation class!)

♦ ♦ ♦ ♦ ♦ ♦

The year I was a sophomore, Senior Skip Day was outrageous to the point of disgusting. Some road signs and various junk such as a playground turtle and some Indian statues from a park were dumped on the school's front steps; wire was run through locker holes; eggs were smashed all over the campus; seniors were sleeping in the parking lot, and eight kids were thrown into the pond. I was appalled at such rowdy behavior, but thought nothing of attending rowdy concerts, and going often. My dad was a champ and drove my buddies and me to many shows out of town, but he was not as cool to us as he thought he was. On one such drive he advocated for short hair on boys. "Even Rick Jager has short hair," Dad noted. We were on a trip to Springfield, Massachusetts in a car packed with teenage boys sporting long hair.

"Dad, you mean Mick Jagger." I was utterly embarrassed.

After one concert I wrote that *a surge of people mobbed the doors to get in and my friends and I were swept off our feet. It was frightening not to feel the floor. I was then stuck behind a glass door lookin' into the face of a policeman. One policewoman had tons of pipes in her hand from unlucky kids' pockets.*

After my friend Libby and I went to one show I commented, *We couldn't sit and listen to the next group – we took off and ran outside and raced around and screamed until there was no place to go. No drug, I don't think, will ever make me feel that good.*

It turned out though that a drug did make me feel good, and I began using dope to help me cope. Things had become very tense at our house. My mom had been sleeping in the guestroom for quite some time and *had a book on divorce in her room. There was a big* fight; Dad slammed doors and hollered and swore at Mom. She talked about condos. I usually liked to listen at the top of the stairs but was too scared this time. I felt sick, but they must feel weird. Dad's immaturity and insensibility control his actions. He is unhappy with practically all of the home/life factors and takes it out on us. This bullshit scene between Mom and Dad has continued for so long that I have become numb. On the outside I functioned properly by getting good grades and making it into the National Honors Society. I learned how to suppress. On the inside I was a great believer in "stuffing," and had perfected the skills of crying silently and yelling onto paper. My journal was the safe place to complain, rant, judge and question. This partial release through diary venting gave me some respite, but I found an added escape in smoking pot. The drug expanded my limited vision of myself and it worked well as stress relief. I also liked how it smelled. I suppose I thought that since liquor was an accepted drug at home and commonly used there, I wasn't being too far out of line for using marijuana.

When homework didn't bury me, I often took a joint to the woods across the street after school, and then watched "The Mickey Mouse Club" on TV for jollies. No one else was home then. The drug made me more peaceful and inspired about everything, even math and history (when I wasn't feeling paranoid, that is). I took precautions to cover up my drug use by washing hands, chewing gum and putting Visine™ in my eyes. Sometimes I needed to call upon my inner actress to play the role of a straight person in front of my mom when she returned home. My diary captured some typical highs-- *I was stoned and staring at Lib's dog – it resembled peoples' faces like an Indian chief and Nixon and a witch, even a mound of red ants. Al was lookin' at us like we were balding or something. Last weekend when I was high at a show I was asked for gum – it felt like forever feeling in my purse. I said it was all gone because I couldn't find it, but there had been 4 packs left!!!*

Somehow my brother Scott and I managed to get away with smoking bongs in the crawlspace in his room that he had converted into a "den." Dad commented that Scott's room smelled like pot but I assured Dad that he was detecting the smell of dirty socks.

I was sneaking around and getting high, but I wasn't creating many problems for our parents...except for the time I lied to Mom about going bowling with some friends. I went to a popular party spot in a big open field instead. *Kathy and I partied with Craig – his friend asked if we wanted to do some hash so we good-naturedly agreed.* Mom peeked at my diary the next day and found out that our driver to the party was stoned and needed encouragement to stay awake and not swerve. (Note: angel intervention acknowledged!) Mom was not lenient when it came to important issues like safety, and she properly punished me.

Only once did I go to school under the influence of alcohol. Since beverages were allowed in class, I brought in a bottle of OJ secretly mixed with vodka. School was a blast that day. When I got high though, I had a tougher time being relaxed around people, so smoking pot before school was out of the question. I was paranoid even when I was straight and had frequent yucky episodes of insecurity like this one: *Attacked by fierce paranoia today – I absolutely hate it when it comes. It was due to my believing myself to be ugly and that what I was wearing wasn't attractive. It was awful and always is! An intense lack of confidence... This year I have been more unconcerned, since worrying about appearances is such a waste of time. I remember (in 9th grade) how I'd always be so self-conscious that I couldn't eat in the café.* (Maybe it was due to having braces.)

Not only did I fear eating in front of others, I was also extremely uneasy sleeping in the presence of others as well. I didn't like closing my eyes in front of anyone; I would never go to sleep on planes or buses, and if on a car trip, I would bury my face somewhere. If confronted with having to be uncomfortably honest with someone---you know me---I preferred writing notes whenever possible to avoid having a strained conversation.

Despite these various neuroses, I still liked myself. *I wonder if it's characteristic of being psychologically disabled that I enjoy my own company to the extent that I do.*

FALLING FOR A HANDSOME LOSER

My focus at sixteen, as it was when I was ten, was on a guy's incredible good looks. I continued to view cute boys as art objects, and I could be mesmerized by the design of their faces.

For several summers I worked in Maine at the previously mentioned church camp, an ideal setting for young love to sprout. I fell headlong for Dave. He was gorgeous with a nice firm chest, good teeth, a hearty laugh, and an overall charisma unfortunately clouded by frequent bad moods. He worked as the chef's assistant and I often worked on the dining hall crew. My heart fluttered whenever he was in view, his white uniform complementing his dark summer tan. While bundling silverware into napkins or mopping the massive floor, I enjoyed listening to the cooks joke and complain about working. I liked how Dave formulated puns within seconds and made speeches by presidents in different voices (usually after work when he was blitzed). We flirted during the day and hung out in the evenings, which mostly consisted of my watching him drink and horse around with the chef. Part of me craved his company, and another part thought he was psychotic, when he made such comments as, *You're so sexy it scares me. [But, later that night] I see you've got some problems bothering you and I don't want to hear them. Good night. (He thought he was the center of everything.)*

Of course Dave could come out with some really sweet talk to keep me hooked. We had our first shower together and I couldn't believe how tenderly he spoke. "I'm falling in love with you. Really. It's everything about you; the way you are, the things you do."

"Man, I'm so happy you feel that way." For some reason I had trouble telling him I loved him back. The words refused to come out. I figured if he said something like that later, I could tell him then. Maybe I didn't yet love him because his moods were scary and beer made his temperament much worse. He might have been manic-depressive. Maybe because I was such a suck-up for attention, I was focused more on my mixed feelings and not able to respond appropriately to his affection. On the other hand, his self-absorption did deflect from his attentiveness, particularly after sex when he instantly fell asleep. (We snuck into unoccupied camp dorm rooms.) I would lie there and wonder how long I was supposed to be captive and uncomfortable in his arms. How much nicer it would've been to murmur into each others' ears with that happy glow, that comfort of union, as our blanket.

Summer sped by mercilessly, and leaving behind a lover in another state was oh so tragic. I was miserable not knowing if I would see him much after the summer. *After I had endeavored to extinguish all other hopeful possibilities for a happy ending, he called. I felt like I was in a great love story.* We only got together twice.

There were times when I entertained many fantasies involving Dave. I enjoyed conjuring up daydreams where, in one, my parents brought Dave home for a weekend surprise. Since my fantasy skills had become so developed, I imagined that *I could sense my lover watching from the closet, because, I suppose, I have the desire to see him and have him see me. I must be vain. During these illusions, I put on some great acts. I've always wondered about this: why is it that at certain times, I can feel a person when he's not present?* But, like any sensible girl who could occasionally keep her romantic notions in check, I realized, *Maybe the best thing to do [was] to continue to love him but untie the knot that ties my soul to his. Now the pains of an impractical attachment [were] gone.*

Since the long-distance relationship never sizzled, it fizzled. Regardless, I flourished at projecting that the following summer, I would dazzle him, he would be hopelessly in love with me, and we would become a couple again. When I found that Dave didn't want me the next year, I went through many emotional stages – anger, resentment and hating myself. I even contemplated plunging into the freezing Atlantic one night after his rejection, but he wasn't worth it. It was healthier for me to write a poem instead.

The Dragon and the Maiden

So much has gone unspoken
Too many nights have gone by
I long to hear you speak
in your gentle way
only for me and the moment and
I miss that fine satisfaction
The giving and receiving of thoughts
The very special touching

All recent energies have been put into
finding ways to be near you
For getting closer, the need of attention.
I hope not to revive the past
The senses concentrate on
that you my affections grow for now

I can only remain attentive
to your interests and moods
Waiting, not wanting to bother you
But my heart is tired
The unexpected unresponsiveness
at times closes in, and maybe
I should realize that
your desires lie elsewhere.

When I looked back on my behavior I wished I had responded differently to Dave's moods by being bolder and less obsequious. I wondered if I could have enticed him by being more direct, and I reported, *When I think about how I acted, I want to hurt my body in such a way that the scar will remind me never to be so ignorant again.* I refrained from cutting, but a part of me could relate to girls who use that means to deal with their feelings. If I hadn't brought my feelings out on paper, I might have suffered more.

Coming to my heart's rescue later that summer, a kind and quiet member of the male crew named Tom put romance back in balance and taught me how to trust again. He was sweet, thoughtful and cheerful – a big departure from Dave. I liked how Tom would swing his bright blond hair away from his glasses and how he didn't hold back his upbeat goofiness. We compared our versions of camp work experience, and my tales were far more hilarious. I recounted a few crazy antics by the kitchen crew when we used chickens, cookie dough and pepperoni to make sculpture and act perverted. Tom had been stuck with work that wasn't nearly as entertaining, having the lifeless task of scrubbing out the dumpsters.

Even though the return to high school interrupted our dating, it worked out well that Tom and I lived only about two hours apart in small Connecticut towns. We visited frequently. He patiently taught me to drive a stick shift after my dad gave up on me in frustration. On autumn weekends Tom and I romped around in the woods, and I cracked up when he jumped off rocks and clicked his heels together. We frolicked in apple orchards and basked in the radiance of our tender courtship. We cared not if someone saw him pawing at my chest behind the trees -- amazing how brazen young love can be! I got to be Tom's "love guru" and show him how to be "experienced." One afternoon we were alone in his family's basement rec room, snuggling on the sofa while a football game was on TV. I rapidly massaged the part of him that was like a rocket and it shot off goop somewhere away from the couch. Moments later Tom's dad, with the fantastic name of Iggy (or maybe it was Ziggy, I can't remember which), came down to check on the score of the game. Surely we young lovers projected a nervous energy. Iggy's gaze scanned the room and found a small puddle on the floor. He bent down to investigate and touched it! "What's...this...water doing here?" he remarked. Tom and I went frigid. We had frenzied thoughts about how soon his dad would figure it out. Iggy courteously exited the room without comment.

Tom was easy to love. *I love his expressions. His soft-heartedness. I feel more beautiful than ever before...He wrote with a* twig on my jean leg "I love you." After visiting he said, "I'll write, and I'll call, and I'll miss you." I don't want this to sound like an ordinary love affair, but it's incredible what has developed between us. I thank the Lord for being able to experience such a sweet side of life. Love is a kingdom! I am fully full of happiness for our lives as they now stand together... When Tom and I took a trip to Fitzwilliam, New Hampshire he said, "We must've kissed about 1,000 times." On the hill in a wet snow-shower he blurted out, "I really love you!"

WORDS ON PAPER MADE IT SAFER

Now that I had achieved a little more maturity, my writing became more philosophical. It was cathartic, poetic, and overall cheap therapy. I discovered that I felt lost when I didn't write. I even felt guilty if I ignored those inner prompts to write, as if I were betraying a part of myself whose confidences I chose to invalidate. Confessing my secrets to the diary made me feel more accepting of myself. Writing made me face the darkness that lurked around my heart and then helped me return to my center. The scribbles and exclamations were the starting point for an emerging self-awareness, evident in my writing, *I sat up in bed and realized who I am. My mind lately tends to yield to scientific brainstorms and intense thinking rather than to mild states of confusion and brief periods of silliness. I discovered that my acting and role-playing all have to do with the way I'd like people to look at me. Is that myself, though, or someone I've seen in the movies?*

Having read my earlier entries made me remember how good I can express – how well I can feel – through writing. It's funny how I feel when I pick up my journal, it's like stepping inside myself. I ought to remember how therapeutic it is for me to write out my feelings.

There was also something synergistic when a picture bubbled up from the mud of my mind and words started jockeying around, floating into the position of sensible thought. Writing was a pleasurable science, the chemistry of pen to paper creating substance. Sometimes my mind was so clear, the words would pop up like in a Magic 8 Ball™. Or, the writing itself would surprise me with its brutal honesty that rang so true, hitting a note inside me, like a finger stroking a crystal goblet and achieving a perfect pitch. But I also wrote because I was accustomed to being quiet while growing up and keeping things inside. Even though it wasn't often that I spoke up, I noticed that people didn't always hear me – when I voiced an opinion, others seemed so focused upon what they needed to express that my words dissolved like soap leaves. Maybe I learned not to bother trying to be heard, or perhaps it hurt too much to talk, for I remember the painful way my braces used to scrape across my gums and I had to keep putting wax in my mouth. The act of observing and writing certainly taught me to be a good listener, at least.

Perhaps it was due to my having cleared up many issues by writing, or perhaps it was timing, but during my senior year I had completely lost my sense of paranoia. No longer having braces was a big plus and having landed Tom was an added boon. However, *I had to fight for my sanity in school because I hated it (with a passion). I was no longer interested in the study of anything.* Now questioning the value of what I was learning, school seemed like a big waste of time. The demons of doubt and darkness wound round me and I noticed how they piped their poison into me, luring me into suicidal thoughts, but I had the proper sense to shush those voices up.

Getting through school day after day was a struggle but another good-looking guy pleasantly distracted me. (Having Tom as an out-of-town boyfriend didn't stop me from flirting with the locals.) Scott was a tall dark dude with striking blue eyes who was on the football team AND was the coolest of cool. He had a sexy way of moving his strong body around in the halls, simply oozing divine masculinity. Thrill of thrills, I played the staring game in math class with him. Did I start it first? *I always like to count how many looks I can get – once I scored 8! When Scott went to sharpen his pencil I was right behind him. I cannot describe his gorgeousness, just that he is a creature to behold. This sounds so corny, but my mind just goes crazy when I picture that face lookin' at me!* The game didn't amount to anything though and I remained loyal to Tom. Occasionally he and I had trouble keeping the conversation going when we talked on the phone. I hated those spaces of silence and racked my brain to find a topic to spill into the quiet while he waited, not volunteering much from his end. My awkward communication blips with Tom were in stark contrast to the normal phone calls I heard my friend Alison have with her boyfriends. I envied the way she was on the phone with them for long periods, while giggling and eating salad, sitting on the kitchen floor, with the long phone cord dangling nearby. I would not be able to count how many times I called her phone number to find it busy for hours!

In part I credit angelic forces for getting me safely to the age of eighteen. I never crashed my Dodge Dart, even though I drove stoned part of the time, and didn't wreck the VW bug I had later, despite sliding off ice patches in the winter and letting my back bumper kiss a few mailboxes. To celebrate my birthday, our parents let Scott and me hold a big keg party in the back yard. *300 people showed up! It was ego-boosting to go up to the kegs and brag that I'm hostess and don't need to defend my unstamped hand. Checked on classmate cutie Scott – he was off doin' something close to stumbling. Fences were busted. Tom and I cleaned up the yard the next day from 5:30-8:00 am, and it had looked like a dump. When I was "policing the grounds" I found 1 shoe, a mayo jar, 2 shirts and a package of papers.* It was during this party that one of the tipsy participants mistook the extra frig downstairs for a toilet and peed in it. Can you believe that? Dad, you cleaned it out I think. Thanks.

At any rate, college was just around the corner, and even though I was ready to get away from home, the thought of making that big jump weighed heavily on me. Having to come up with a college major, I stated that *this whole business is a fuck-up! I pity every senior who ever was and ever will be. College is all I ever worry about now!* There were so many things to think about as well as copious unanswered questions. The stress of moving into adulthood necessitated exploration and release, and journaling was my solution. *I probed myself in character and found it scary but helpful. At times I deeply wish to be changed – I battle within myself against 2 personalities. I go far inside and lose my happiness and come out with uncomfortable thoughts that stir my troubled emotions... I am growing up (and it is very strenuous). I try to be open to both renewing and exchanging. I guess being sensitive is what makes me what I am.*

Mom admitted she is an alky and I hope I do not "catch" it. [All I remember now is that Mom drank to relax and get to sleep. She did not become volatile. Today she is a non-boozing fitness fanatic.]

KELLY'S ROCK N' ROLL REVIEW FROM THE 70'S

Marshall Tucker Band - gave 4 encores, about 30 minutes each!

Aerosmith – best concert ever – overwhelmingly impressive

Johnny Winter – he was SO good on guitar, it was unreal

Rick Derringer – had holes cut out of his jeans so that you saw his butt cheeks

KISS – stage explosions, smoke coming out of guitars, jumping up & down in huge platform shoes

Jethro Tull – I was poked in the eye with a joint (the eye with the contact lens)

Boston – excellent, simply excellent

Yes - UNBELIEVABLE – lead singer Jon looked and sounded celestial as the band played on a rotating stage

Kansas – my all-time favorite group rocked it big time

Note: I saw about 20 more performers but those listed here are the most memorable.

I hope this bit of trouble at home doesn't cause me to lose that will and that caring that I have. It gets hard trying to understand life and I've been looking for as many little bits of gladness I can find.

My youth is so special to me right now – so many times have I recently looked down at my jean-clad legs, their shadows walking in the winter sun, and I think, "How young I am!"

I heard in drama class that most writers are "touched!"

I think that I like myself a lot more than others ever will. How come I worry too much about being normal?

I wonder how my past brought me up to this point – I mean, how I became shaped into this personality. In relating my childhood to present character, I am sure my hostility to my father stems back from certain events but I fail to pinpoint them. I try at times to generate forgiveness but my efforts are lost in hopelessness. There was once a period of near-affection between us and it had been satisfying to feel compatibility. But the last four months have been useless for true, healthy communication. It's sad and depressing. I wish that his learning to love himself came easier. The situation is almost always tense, the whole scene wrong. I want to help – but the problem is too overwhelming to find a beginning.

I can't help talking to myself when I'm alone – it just makes the trip quite a bit more interesting if I strike up some conversation with my other me.

For a while today I thought I really was crazy, spending so much uneventful time by myself. You know, finding myself staring at doorknobs and light bulbs – just plain weirdness. I did enjoy a great sunset – it was like a sandbar in the sky with all those cloud patches, like puffs of corrugated fingerprints.

Tom and I are so tight and I will always have this kind of love to keep as proof of a fulfilled life. (But I did say to Lib, "Isn't it too bad that life just isn't as romantic as you dream it to be?")

POETRY BREAK

On my daily morning pilgrimage into the hills
I greet the day feeling peaceful, despite the annoying flap of my jeans
where my flat butt fails to fill out the space.
I think of the birds as my friends.
I think of the flowers as my mentors.

DESPAIR AND DISPARAGEMENT

Tragedy is full of mystery. It can suck you into its cyclone, spit you out feeling exhausted and deeply disturbed, and make you an instant seeker of the meaning of life. So many vital questions can remain perplexing.

A dear friend of mine had to face the tragic experience of getting pregnant her very first time, just like Juno. Our teenage minds struggled with trying to understand why God had selected her for this awful lesson. The upset was terrible, but what was five million times worse was when a close family friend was murdered. Kim was only nineteen. I could barely believe the horrifying details, and it seemed as if my resistance to accepting Kim's death meant, for a second, that the story couldn't be real. I wanted to push the images out of my head, out of the chopping block of reality, so that Kim would still be alive.

Kim shared an apartment with her boyfriend Donnie. One evening after an argument, Donnie went out and had not returned home when Kim went to bed. A stranger came to her door about 12:30 am, banging at it to be let in, and Kim sleepily opened her door, thinking it was Donnie without his key. Kim struggled with the intruder and screamed, yet no one came to save her life. Blood was all over the place. This freak on drugs also sexually assaulted her. He had told a friend earlier that he "was going to get her."

Just a year or two before, in a high school play, Kim had acted the role of a young woman who was murdered. I had asked her how she felt about having that role or if it was hard, and Kim replied that the drama interested her. Every time I recalled that conversation I felt eerie, and I daydreamed that time had been reversed and that Kim wasn't gone. Whenever I suffered a simple wound in the kitchen I imagined her attacker's knife slicing her deeply, and I felt aghast at how much pain I felt when touched by one little knife, when she was repeatedly cut with a larger weapon.

I have pondered Kim's death and used it as a touchstone for

formulating questions about God, picturing the brutal scene over and over. As an adult I have often brought the incident to mind whenever I felt fearful for the world, for my kids and myself. The murder validated the negative comments my ego regularly whispered that kept me in fear - those quiet utterances that make humans think they are separate from one another.

I played the song "Bless the Beasts and Children" on my recorder at Kim's memorial service, forcing myself to maintain an even flow of breath and keep the melody smooth; glancing into the pews would have caused an instant breakdown, and I had trouble blowing air over the big lump in my throat. Now that Kim was slain, I had to accept that the world was no longer the same as I had pretended to believe.

Kim's mom, Coral, later gave me some of the things that once belonged to the girl we mourned. We sat quietly on my bed, both finding little to say. I plaintively accepted these objects, feeling so misplaced by grief. The pain we felt clearly radiated from our eyes. I thought about how devastating it must have been for Kim's parents to first enter the room that would never again be occupied by their beloved daughter. They would sit among the books she had read, as well as those they had read to her as a young child. Through tears they would look at the pictures of her classmates on the walls, and sort through old letters from boyfriends. They would tenderly hold the trinkets Kim had collected from vacations, and inhale her scent that still lingered in the closet. Their memories just weren't enough, and these two parents would suffer from holes blasted into their hearts that could never really heal.

Not only did Coral experience the horrible tragedy of Kim's murder, she had also buried Kim's adopted brother Chris just two years prior. An unusual car accident took his life at seventeen. It was entirely heart wrenching to lose Kim and Chris but maybe even more so to watch Coral's body deteriorate after her children's deaths. She has since led a painful life with crippling arthritis and other maladies, relying on the constant aid of doctors, drugs, wheelchairs, surgeries and her husband Bob's tireless care. I have hated that this beloved woman's life has been filled with repeated suffering. Even recently, she lost part of a leg due to gangrene. Yet, Coral has continued to sprinkle her darling, cheery laugh and British accent into my life when we talk long-distance, and together we delight in birds, flowers, fairies and other magical things. Acting as her and Bob's surrogate daughter has been a great honor.

♦ ♦ ♦ ♦ ♦ ♦ ♦

Back at home, about thirty years ago, my parents had their own emotional wounds to deal with. They had fired off enough ammo at each other that they finally called it quits and separated. The family crisis was described as this: *Dad moved out tonight. It was sad as Scott was helping him pack some things – my father was crying, lightly. And then I realized, Jesus, it's not fair that Mom always swayed me into believing that he was so evil. I listened to him too, naturally, but what he said was always touched with sorrow and confusion, while she referred to him with bitterness and resentment. I can't blame her, but I also admire the efforts he made. Tonight she holed herself up in the basement to be away from him while he discovered that none of his shirts had been ironed...*

Life was giving me plenty of opportunities to make emotional adjustments, but at last I could see salvation in the form of liberty from home and high school. *School is coming to a close. I'm no longer a dreamy freshman – in turn I'm a growing adult whose life is fuller and fuller. And it still bothers me to see how quick living is - the day clicks off too soon and the past seems illogical and there's a fat inchworm sliding up the cord of my clock-radio. I know that although the future is so near, it seems it'll never get here. I'm gonna miss this way of living, this room where I've done so much thinking and dancing and writing – in this town I'm gonna leave behind all my childhood fancies and phone numbers and long friendships.*

A funny thing happened at the Senior Prom. While getting up from the table, I stepped on the front of my halter dress and gave everyone a free show! The dress had no built-in bra so there I was, just for a few seconds, standing among my peers and flashing my chest, and Tom and the others didn't even notice.

After my last day of high school, I commented, *All my posters are down, and I could get very sad if I wanted to, yet there is so much life ahead of me.* Before we parted amicably and headed off to separate colleges, Tom and I went back to camp one last time. That final summer in Maine gave me much to write about. Concerning previous lover/loser Dave, I vented, *it had gotten to the point that I would cringe at his voice and wince at his drunken laugh. I had been reading back on some very early diary pages, and still I cannot believe myself. I was so hooked on Dave, not knowing what he'd become, thriving on memories and expectations. I learned the hard way...* What was more, he bugged the hell out of me when he taunted me in front of everyone, mocking me by saying, "I'm sorry" repeatedly in a high squeaky voice.

Even though I had long since given him up, I couldn't help feeling absolutely tormented and disgusted the time I heard Dave and Jenni screwing in the room next door of the girls' quarters. He thought he was so bloody charming, climbing up onto the roof of the cottage and going in through Jenni's window. (They weren't dating, you see, but were both sloshed from a crew party.) I wondered for two hours if the pair had any idea I was right there, not moving or making a sound--frozen yet burning at the same time. Jenni became the first person that I couldn't stand; Dave had never acted that way with me!

Despite the annoyances from Mr. Former Heartthrob that final summer before college, there were the joys of playful unabashed youth. My journal captured a random food fight: *I threw beans at Dudley, he threw water on me, I put soapsuds on Skep, he nailed me with Ajax, I had flour in my hair, then butter – we all ran straight into the ocean to wash off our various weapons.* No doubt this playfulness occurred after my kitchen shift when I had stood for three hours washing pots. (I wonder what was on the menu that day!) Our silly kitchen crew was still immature enough to be tickled every day when one old lady would ask someone to please open her bottle of prune juice.

Good Fortune Cookie saying:
Avert misunderstanding by being calm,
poised and balanced."

ONE OF MY FAVORITE QUOTES
"The world is so full of a number of things, I'm
sure we should all be as happy as kings."
Robert Louis Stevenson

UNDER THE DORM ROOF

It didn't appeal to me to attend my dad's alma matter in Kentucky since it was so far from home, so I picked the University of Rhode Island. It was close to my hometown but far enough away. Little did I realize that I had selected a school whose state in 1977 consumed the highest percentage of alcohol in the United States. Beer was too bitter for my taste, but some of the boys on my floor drank it often. One night I noticed that co-ed Alan was definitely "zooed," and he was walking into rooms asking if any girls wanted to "bundle." The males that I thought had the best nicknames were Buns, Bugs, Bo, Biscuit, Mudhead and Nurse. Some of these goofballs indoctrinated me into "freshmanism" by telling me I had a phone call in the hall and then drenching me with two buckets of water.

College food was a serious concern for me. I despised the salad that came from huge bags and smelled like chemicals, and after tasting a few of the greasy, flat cafeteria hamburgers, I could no longer bring myself to eating them. They assaulted my eyes and turned my stomach. It was thus an easy decision for me to become a strict vegetarian, and I have continued as one for thirty healthy years. (My poor mother won't ever forget the time she cooked up some live lobsters at home when I was still in high school. Once I heard the desperate squealing sounds coming from the pot of boiling water, I cried my eyes out on the front steps. My sensitivity to creatures certainly contributed to the ease with which I chose to be vegetarian.)

In spite of all the essays I had to produce for college, I didn't abandon my diary. I always felt better after writing about things. Writing was an ever-present source of comfort. A shiny mirror! An inner probe! I reflected, *I just realized that I create my own problems and instability. I havta free myself from the ties of anyone else. Too often I concern myself with so many people who are insignificant to me. I really have to tell myself not to feel under the eyes of onlookers. Other days I'd feel a surge of joy constantly rising in me – it made me wonder if, being so happy, I was absolutely loony...*

My parents divorced once I was in college, so I got to spend holidays with two spiteful people in separate states. For Thanksgiving I visited my dad in Connecticut and just had to snicker when he yelled, "Fuck you!" at a football game on TV. When celebrating Christmas Eve in Kentucky with my mom, I joined a gang of relatives and cruised over to a house decorated with a flashy Elvis poster on their roof. We all sang "Blue Christmas" from the curb and a kid with a shotgun came to the door to run us off. At the midnight church service my aunt asked my mom if she was taking Communion and Mom replied, "I don't think I could eat another bite." This quip set the pew to shaking as we women could barely stop giggling during the mass. I enjoyed my relatives' perky company and particularly got a kick out of their twangy speech and the way they said "dudn't" instead of doesn't.

Back at school after vacation, I experienced the harsh winter storm known as the Blizzard of 1979 that hit several states in the northeast. *2000 cars were left abandoned on a turnpike, the dining hall ladies had to camp out in the dorm, and my friend Richard skiied on the beach! It was a miserable walk to classes when they were in session; it was so cold it hurt.*

It is surprising to look back and observe that I documented severe weather but didn't detail in my journal the heat wave I felt around Michael. He was the sexiest thing I ever met and my first college romance. He entranced me when he took his long brown hair out of his ponytail; it was clean, gorgeous and hung smoothly over his lanky body. His penetrating blue eyes turned me into a weak-kneed wuss. I remember making the first move, asking Michael in class if he knew it was the birthday of a popular guitarist. Our cheery little chat opened a door that I gladly flung myself through to get to know him more intimately.

Michael stole my heart by blowing a mean blues harmonica, pouring his Irish soul into the notes. I played for him in return; one evening while waiting for him for two hours on the roof, I went through every melody I knew on my recorder, feeling distraught by his nonappearance. The times that Michael did come around we frequented blues bars in Providence and rock concerts on campus, or spent nights alone together in his grandmother's quaint seaside bungalow near the university. In general he preferred lying down to standing up, so if given the opportunity to flop on a bed, he would get comfortable and quietly command, "Come here." Was that sexy or what? I eagerly placed my body tight up against his. Not only did he have huge sex appeal, he also was a good conversationalist, and as a rule I fell for men with good vocabularies. Sometimes Michael cleaned fish on the docks in Newport, but his fantastic body felt so heavenly next to mine that I easily ignored the distinct smell.

Michael may have loved me but he already had a girlfriend away at a private school. (He didn't divulge this information about Denise right away.) My competitor dropped in sometimes, popping my bubble of love and taking him away from me; she eventually won out. I wasn't the kind of girl who was loose and groovy with his having another lover—as a Taurus I wanted to possess him all to myself. I'll never forget the time Denise showed up at a club where Michael and I were dancing with friends. She tapped him on the shoulder and they promptly left. I felt so abandoned and my heart sank when I realized we wouldn't be cuddling later that night. His departure hurt so much I had to go outside and wrestle with my anger and shock. Overwhelmed, and under the influence of alcohol, I threw myself onto the ground to cry. I used the protection of a car to shield me so as not to be seen in my tender state. Cold and upset, I waited for my friends to give me a ride home, wondering how Michael would interact with me later, curious about what comments he might make. (Sorry reader, I don't remember the outcome! Whatever the case, I didn't want to shun Mr. Magnetism.) The school year ended soon enough, but I was content to let our relationship be weird and wonderful while it lasted that freshman year.

Now when I return to the sweeter thoughts about him, I feel like I am opening a magic treasure box that will be safe forever. A friend mentioned that Michael had put on some weight years later, but I can keep him thin and spectacular in my mind. I can still hear his Rhode Island accent and remember the awesome view we shared from a beach on Cape Cod. That magic box contains precious memories that I am lucky to own, and these words help to preserve them through time.

GREAT QUOTES
"In a man's happiness God is glorified."
Khalil Gibran

"With our thoughts we make the world."
Buddha

LOVING AND LEAVING

Volunteering as a disc jockey for the college radio station as a sophomore gave me several chances to meet new guys. (My radio name was SweetPea). In a meeting of new recruits I spotted Peter who was a brown-haired look-alike of Jesus. His cherubic face contorted in a funny way when he was amused. He also had an eye tooth that poked out of his wide smile which I found appealing. Peter had a thin frame, good posture and a calm demeanor. His suave radio voice soothed my nerves, helping me to be daring and thus test the waters of the boy-girl game with him. On the prowl, I tracked the pattern of what time Peter left the radio station so that I could innocently intercept him outside on the patio. Our friendship developed slowly, for he appeared to be socially stunted around women. Once I had gained his trust he began bringing me fabulous rhododendrons from his grandparents' garden. We talked into the wee hours getting to know each other. We slept on the beach a few times, even though the waves were terribly loud, and we woke up with sandy ears and clothes damp with dew. I was thrilled when Peter told me that I had "loads and loads of good karma."

When he showed up for a dinner date one evening I told him, "Peter, you look really good tonight." He was quite adorable in the flannel shirts he wore, particularly when his long hair wasn't in a ponytail.

"You've looked good to me for a long time." My eyebrows lifted in surprise.

Our relationship brought us both many gifts—he turned me on to some great guitarists, taught me some astrology and instructed me in raising happy houseplants; I cared for him in ways that his family had not achieved. Peter was emotionally deprived, frequently left on his own due to a sister's chronic illness. *He comes from a family afraid of and cold to expressing love. They are people in boxes, so closed to*

41

warmth. They made him cautious about showing his love to others. His family didn't even give him anything for his birthday or for graduation. I worked with Peter on his pain and "buried material" – we pulled out more and more of his feelings. I felt like I was a true friend and comrade.

How would I have known I would meet such a darling dude after I had already committed to transferring to a different college? My mom convinced me that Indiana University had more to offer me for studying communications, and I liked the idea of being able to visit her more often in Kentucky. The days prior to my departure were so distressing that I wrote, *I was upset almost beyond control. It can be really hard to be happy sometimes – my heart does break now and then.* The Joni Mitchell songs we listened to made me even more melancholy.

Dejected, I parted from my sweetheart and moved to Indiana. In order to cope with my lovesickness, I took up the spiritual path of meditating in an ashram and foregoing drugs. Aside from attending the daily evening meditation with the Swami or another teacher, I also participated in an occasional Saturday "Long Meditation." This gathering lasted about seven hours, most of which was spent sitting, with a few silent walks thrown in for stretching. Quite often I exper-ienced the powerful energy flow that was transmitted from sage to student; Swami would tap me gently on the forehead (the seat of the "third eye") and I was nearly knocked over by the force of the intense energy generated by his fingertips. Some students did fall backwards from their lotus position into the lap of the person behind them, not from falling asleep, but from receiving a dose of Swami's potent, electric vibrations. These touches were a quick spiritual fix, a brief installment of bliss. The meditator who received the slumped person into their lap would allow them to rest there until he or she was able to gather their senses and sit back up. (It did seem pretty weird having someone's head in your crotch.) During those moments in the carpeted, shrine-like room when I was centered and clear, my heart felt so expanded that it could have taken a flying leap out of my chest.

This period of self-awakening was rich with inner growth and my journal overflowed with realizations. *Swami asked us, "What's your main goal in life?" and my only answer for that is growing. He made me realize that I wasn't going with the flow of my life, fighting my destiny by being attached to the past. I'm just yearning for more insight, clearer vision and stronger understanding. Swami says the only source of security and stability is inside. Meditation is a time for facing ourselves, and we should pay attention to the choices that we make every minute.*

I feel incredibly happy and walk around almost feeling like I should keep that big grin in. I have also been crying from intense beauty and incredible gratefulness. Some days it's so overwhelming that my happiness comes out in tears. I am intent on keeping this freshness of spirit stored with as many peaceful preservatives as possible.

The pattern of dualities in everything seems clearer--there's an opposite reaction to every action. I get so sick of hearing the devil and the angel in me hassling over every little thing!

Most of Swami's followers seemed like normal folk, but some in his upper echelon were especially charismatic and dynamic. I befriended one of Swami's aides, a married businessman whom I'll call Ted. I wasn't actually attracted to Ted but I did enjoy his friendly, charming manner, as he wasn't one of the more quiet, serious ashram students. Ted and I had a few pleasant chats and he usually made me laugh. I lived around the corner from the ashram and he dropped by for a visit one night. I feel quite certain that I didn't lead him on, but perhaps my naivety gave him the false idea that I would be open to his advances.

Lord knows what kind of horseshit he used to persuade me to bond sexually with him. He must have said something about just wanting to be inside me as some sort of union of higher energy. Even though he told me he would not pursue full intercourse, it only took my body a few minutes to reject what was happening, and I found myself freezing up. My arms went rigid and my hands became curled into tightly balled fists that I could not move for five long minutes. My face muscles were so restricted I could barely talk. Ted promptly bailed and

I was flooded with embarrassment at my poor judgment. Later I would realize that my body responded in this stiff way whenever I unintentionally hyperventilated. Losing muscle control like that gave me a horrible feeling of abandonment, the way I no longer had control over my body; it felt similar to the way my cheek feels rock hard after the dentist has thoroughly numbed my gums.

Okay, so I had a devious spiritual acquaintance and wanted to fink on him. I had a Swami who was rumored to have several lovers. I tried to stick it out at the ashram, be a faithful student and pursue my journey to deep peacefulness, but I was missing Peter like crazy! He had such beautiful handwriting and said such endearing things in his letters that I missed him all the more. In one of his cards he said, "When you consider the short time we've been together, I think it's been good and holds much promise for the future, as long as we both keep love as our main gift to each other."

Since we couldn't stand to be apart, I managed to talk Peter into moving to my new town of Bloomington. We sporadically participated at the ashram and Peter got a job at the bakery that ashram members owned and operated. We proved to be decent roommates, and he didn't mind the pretty rose wallpaper in the sunny room we shared. (Yay, here was a fellow who had not totally suppressed his feminine side. However, I did not know what to think of him when he wore only a sombrero, sunglasses and jockstrap for Halloween). Peter was a good complement to the work I was doing on my nutty idiosyncrasies. He helped me be calm and take more time in what I did, and not to judge myself so critically. He also helped me learn to be especially patient, since he often ran late and I was forced to waste time waiting for him.

Peter and I came together as spiritual partners to help heal our wounds. He evidently needed me more for psychological and emotional reasons than physical ones. Although I was deeply attracted to him, he on the other hand didn't dole out the lovemaking. *Peter's withholding of sex challenged my Taurean addictions for security. We would go a month without sex. Close to 95% of my remembered dreams involve being sensual with my lover. This type of dream* behavior has been occurring without fail for nearly 6 months. Obviously my sleeping Self wants to do what my waking Self cannot.

◆ ◆ ◆ ◆ ◆ ◆ ◆

Not only had Peter joined me, but my brother Scott also came to Indiana as well to attend the university. Scott and I took a Wildflower and Edible Plants class and went on a spring weekend retreat. Being the earth sign of Taurus, I already felt strongly connected to dirt, flowers, trees and rocks. I felt overjoyed to learn the plant varieties of the mountain laurel, lady slippers, squirrelcorn, bulbous buttercup, trout lily, spring beauty, showy orchid and the pawpaw tree. We learned that dandelion is four times more nutritious than lettuce. Prior to the retreat there had been fourteen days of nonstop rain, but getting to tromp around in the drippy forests made me feel spirited and chirrupy. Even so, trees always seemed to have a power over me that made me feel pensive and reverent. I was drawn in by the beauty and serenity of the forest. My diary bore witness to my love of things growing in nature: *It's a miraculous time because of the spring's artwork. Redbuds and lilacs fill the day with precious color and tree petals fall onto the street looking like bright confetti. The crocuses grace the lawn in full force – they fill my eyes with deep color and my heart greets them with delight. I feel as though I'm living in a three-dimensional Monet painting and am over my head in joy! I get tremendous pleasure from looking at all the colors and patterns everywhere and smelling everything. I am just plumb full of rejoicing!*

Seeing as how egos are skillful at casting shadows, mine often succeeded in dampening all that bubbly joy. Being in a relationship forced me to examine my many hang-ups, and I found some good, painful lessons to be learned in life's Slinky™ of ups and downs. Not having gotten far myself at moving through some of my tougher inner issues like insecurity and self-criticism, I consulted a psychic "reader." This spiritual consultation gave me plenty to ponder. I summarized,

I have a sensitivity to others' energies. I also have such a concern or sympathy for others that I willingly take on their negativity. I want to comfort them so much I take on their tensions... I feel emotions very deeply but seem to repress them. And, I have a very sincere intent to know God, and that desire is the key... I wondered why my happiness is so tied to Peter's and why my self-doubt seems to come from my not having felt accepted by people in the past. I was too shy – I should have vocalized and not held back my feelings. What will ground me is my strength and compassion for my voice inside.

I was thankful for people who could "see." So many had helped me along the way, and their influences allowed me to grow some of that vision for myself. Those little blank books that I kept filling up were my digging tools. I related, *Coming to you, diary, is such a refuge. In reading older diaries I realized that I sure did cling to anyone who really made me feel like I was needed for love! Too bad I spent so much energy having hopes about some boy instead of cultivating myself.*

Optimist International advises to "give
so much time to the improvement
of yourself that you have not
time to criticize others."

WANDERLUST

Peter and I thought that after my college graduation it would be jolly good fun to drive a van out west to Washington, with our ultimate destination being a commune we considered joining. This hippie community was located near Santa Barbara, California, not far from John Travolta's ranch. We headed to the Rainbow Festival in upper Washington with great enthusiasm, now that we were free spirits hitting the road with the world at our wheels. The Rainbow Festival was primarily a gathering of New Age wisdom seekers and loosy-goosy freeloading airheads. I guess I belonged to both groups: I was doing a lot of cosmic, spiritual reading, but I also believed in the rhythm method for birth control, combined with using visualization to keep a spirit from entering my womb. (I had read it works. Well, lucky for me in that regard that Peter was not very sexual.)

During the trip I made a pact with the Great Creator: *Near the border between Colorado and Wyoming I begged God to make me a deal and never let me run over an animal (like prairie dogs).* There had been so many creatures by the side of the road that I was petrified of hitting one. God came through on the deal and I have felt forever indebted (although I still don't remember what my specific part of the bargain was). When we arrived at the festival I felt misplaced and intimidated—so many of the campers liked to parade around in the nude. Many of them had adopted "cosmic" names, like Star Song Rainbow or Indigo Elfin Moonchild. Not only were gobs of hippies thronging the wilderness for a week, but there were also freaks and weirdos who liked to sit nearby the open showers and watch the women bathe. Despite the air of love and transformation, the festival was simply nuts for a person like me who didn't enjoy crowds or exposed bouncy body parts.

The good:

On-site granola making, bread baking

On-site sprout kitchen

The "Sister Circle" where women sang & danced

The healing workshops and free massages

The massive group of people Ohming in a meadow

The bad:

7 mile walk to the main camp

Very low level of hygiene

Had to go potty over a big open pit

Oatmeal every morning

6 camp cases of serious diarrhea

After a few days of trying to avoid using the potty pit dug in the ground, we platonic lovebirds then made our way down the coast of California, happy to be using real toilets and exploring the plentiful beauty of the region. *The ocean there looked like it didn't belong on earth – it had such a celestial appearance, a supreme glow shining thru the sparkly blues. We had been looking for a nice rest spot and found one near some rocks on a cliff overlooking the sea. There were resplendent flowers and I took them as a sign of welcome. We were snugglin' like happy hamster hobbits in our van one night when suddenly I noticed tears on Peter's face. He was feeling the deep beauty of the love we share for each other, and the goodness of it really touched his heart.* Peter and I were also happy to have a real house to shower in when we visited a family we had met at the Festival. Gwilym and Hokulea were the gentlest hippies you could ever meet. They proclaimed that their small son Evergreen was Bing Crosby reincarnated. Gwilym enjoyed playing a game with people that was dubbed "the face game." To play, two people sit across from each other in comfortable positions. They simply stare into each other's eyes. The game is to take as much time as necessary to see into the layers of a face and into one's soul. Gwilym explained that you could see a person's past lives come forward. When I did this experiment with him, I swore that I saw an elderly Japanese sage in his face. When Hokulea and Peter were paired for the game, she was convinced that he had been a Romanian peasant (as had I; we had been lovers before!). Curious, don't you think?

◆◆◆◆◆◆◆

Echoes of Heaven

Today I wore bells around my waist
Feeling foolish, feeling beautiful
Angels walked with me in sound
Playing like a child reminds me
The bright happy world within
My memory, my highest dreams

Finally running out of money near Santa Barbara, Peter and I resigned to ending our trip and start searching for jobs, but it had been so much more fun driving around! We had visited the commune but decided to reject it as our new home, since couples were not allowed to room together. The universe gave us a shared position of live-in attendant for a woman with MS named Karen. We took turns caring for her around the clock and we had a room of our own in her small apartment. Karen was confined to a wheelchair and her speech was slow and slurred. She was very heavy to lift onto her bed and the toilet. In fact she was so disabled that I had to change Karen's tampons. In the middle of the night Peter and I would awake to her calls for help to use the bathroom, or to get her off the floor and back onto the bed. *Poor Karen would cry a lot, even over mundane things like there not being any lettuce.*

We didn't last six months doing that kind of selfless work. Peter and I found our own apartment and other employment that was less draining. We grew a fantastic garden together and mushroom compost was the key. The squash grew big enough for a museum. *Look at what a seed the world is that God planted!*

Regardless of how our plants were flourishing, our relationship life cycle was near its end. We were having some challenging interpersonal communications. Peter was still graciously mirroring back to me my limitations and self-deprecating patterns. I struggled with jealousy; since Peter had such a sweet face and a big heart, he tended to attract the opposite sex. I complained, *I don't like being so possessive because of the hurt I feel. I feel haunted and afflicted by the same gloom that has attacked me for years. I guess if I were more tuned in to my "pool of quiet deep" I would not experience such self-despair. I'm so amazed by my lack of confidence, my apologizing for myself, my smallness... Why haven't I felt good about myself so often?*

When I communed with my brighter side, I mused, *I realized every moment has something to teach! I want to increase my capacity to love by making stronger my ability to forgive. I really want to get to the point that I manifest in my body the real Spirit within me. I want to glorify God's image in me, to become or bring out the beauty which He put there as Himself.*

After four years, Peter and I decided to dissolve our coupleship. It was bizarre to think about how our plans for the future had fizzled like sparks flying away from a campfire. I was extremely bothered that he didn't seem upset, yet I felt so sick from breaking up that I couldn't work for two days. Even though I finally became less fearful of being without him, the split disturbed me so much that I had two tidal wave dreams in a row. In my vulnerable state I also suffered from nastier-than-usual PMS. *How strange that the Lord had to make such a connection with menstrual cycles and feeling LOW. I just keep that same cold expression on my face, and that same dulled look in my eyes. I suspect my period is soon to come because of my emotional dip.*

"Self-condemnation strengthens guilt
which is one of the greatest obstacles on
the path of realization."
Sri Swami Rama (not my particular Swami)

QUIRKY AND WORKING

Long ago when I was young, strong, out of college and needing money, I worked as a housekeeper/helper for seniors and the disabled. One day all I did for two hours was clean a bathtub. It couldn't have been cleaned for years, as it took an excruciating amount of scrubbing and I wanted it perfect before I left. Had the family put dirty pets in the tub as well, or had it become grimy from their overweight bodies alone? Had they honestly been that lazy that they couldn't bend over with a sponge and cleanser? That job was the worst but not the weirdest. The oddest person for whom I cleaned was a toilet paper collector. This very old lady had upwards of sixty rolls in her linen closet. She seemed to treasure her cache. She certainly didn't feel like she had enough because I noticed that toilet paper was on her shopping list.

My batch of old folks was a kaleidoscope of personalities. One gentleman was quite elderly and his dear wife wasn't able to care for him very well. The woman asked me one day if I could help bathe him. I pleaded ignorance about the personal task and declined, but the sweet lady still baked me the most delicious and unforgettable zucchini bread. Another client I quickly became endeared to was a woman with the catchy name of Toby Oberg. She was gifted with an ability to do automatic writing. She spontaneously wrote down what she heard in her head, and this writing was often love letters from a soul in another dimension. She and I talked about the spirit world and other intriguing subjects. Two of my clients were much younger. Jerry was a sad quadriplegic with greasy hair. He grumbled about nearly everything. Suzie was a young rich housewife whose loneliness drove her to pull me off-task to chat about life's mysteries.

When I stop and look at many of the jobs I've had, I feel ashamed by my persistent pattern of flakiness. I was fired from one waitressing job because the owner found out I bought pot from his son. I was let go from another waitressing job because the boss didn't feel confident in my abilities (only once did I spill a piece of pie into a customer's lap). In one of my jobs at a radio station, I kept turning off power to the announcer's microphone to save energy, and forgot to turn it on before he started speaking. Eeeek, the list goes on! In a bakery job, I was told that even though I was considered the best front counter clerk, I needed to be fired because the owners thought I was stealing money from the cash drawer. The problem wasn't that I was pocketing dough (ha) — I just had trouble with the cash register and couldn't balance the receipts with the till. More recently, I walked out on a good job because my supervisor was an eighty-year-old bossy boots whose sour moods gave me panic attacks. I suppose I gravitate to writing because I am my own boss whose moods I can handle most of the time. My mistakes are instantly corrected in one keystroke.

It made sense though that I blended in well with eccentric seniors and other odd folk. Having a compulsive personality, I haven't been a stranger to being strange. I have to wash both of my hands even if just one is dirty; I simply can't get one hand wet and leave the other dry. Sticky food marks on the microwave drive me crazy and I can't tolerate water spots on the counter or floor. If I feel like I have a rough edge to a cuticle I have to pull and tear at it. Commenting about this old habit years ago I wrote, *I just discovered what symbology there is to my old habit of picking at my fingers – it's a parallel to my picking at myself, at being critical and judgmental.* What is more, I am prone to talking to myself. I might have developed this habit while working many years in a public library where all the old lady librarians talked to themselves. To further compound my list of personality quirks, I almost always let people get in front of me at the grocery store, unless their cart is fuller than mine. My blood pressure even rises if I feel I am holding someone up in general. When attending street fairs, I honestly hate to walk past the vendors selling their wares because I feel sorry for them if I'm not making a purchase to help them out. I turn my compost as gingerly as possible so that I don't disturb the worms. (My sensitivity does go a little overboard.)

You might also consider it odd that I have a clean and a dirty side to my pillowcase. (I do not wash every week like a friend of mine.) My pillowcase is smartly labeled with a mark that indicates the clean side for the days I shower. Being particularly fussy about odors, I hate smelling an icky pillowcase under my head when my hair is clean. And, if eating cake, I simply must cut my piece in half and put the top layer upside down on the bottom layer so that the frosting is in the middle.

You have been patient, dear reader, but we now return to my world back at the age of twenty-three. Regardless of how things smelled on the outside, I still needed to fumigate the toxic waste dump that was my neurotic, insecure mind. Now that Peter and I were no longer together, I had the opportunity to go deeper into myself to clear out some junk. I disclosed, *Because today is the new moon I've been watching myself carefully and trying to make efforts at improving my character. I have been living in past resentments as if the hurt will do some good. I must remember that next time I give of myself, I should not be attached to my action, but simply breathe and watch. I am SO sick of my little games to get attention...*

I didn't have too much time to work on the hazardous material of my emotions, having just met a new lover only three weeks after my breakup with Peter. I spotted Eric at our local "Dance Away" that was held every Friday night at the Unitarian Church. I noticed his good looks right off but couldn't help being amused by the way he was hopping around, instead of making his body look like he was dancing. The typical "Dance Away" provided a great workout to good music, and it was here that we normal dancers would often see those very carefree people who rolled around off each other's backs and on the floor, making their version of art and mirror image movement. Those "loose" people got so much exercise and close contact from their "dancing" that, as you can imagine, they smelled pretty stinky.

Eric was even more of a Jesus figure than my previous boyfriend. He had striking blue eyes, long scratchy blond hair, a furry chest, a full beard and a goofy laugh, and he was passionate about social justice and environmental issues. He usually wore these soft blue t-shirts that commanded me to press my chest into his. In fact he even went by the name Blue, but I'll keep things simple and stick to

Eric. On our first date when we went bike riding, the thought bubble over my head read, "Boy, I will follow you anywhere." We shared a love of hiking and spent many hours in the Santa Barbara mountains. Whenever I spoke to him on the phone I perspired heavily. If I knew he would be coming by, I hoped to lure him to fall for me by dancing soulfully near my window. When amused—-which occurred intermittently—-he made a funny face where he half-rolled his eyes and half-bit his lip, giving him the resemblance of a tipsy chipmunk. Regardless, I had no trouble being instantly smitten by this handsome impassioned activist, and I acknowledged, *It's hard to live in the now when dreamy things happen that make me fantasize about the future. Somehow I have the feeling of great happiness, of release, that a very old dear friend is near again. Thinking of Eric brings ideas of reunion, deep inner harmony – more of a spiritual linking as companions than a physical attraction, although that is very much present too. I feel like he's some very special friend whom I had a quick separation from in an earlier lifetime, because I still experience thoughts of "Wow, together again, ah bliss."*

After dancing we went over to the coffee house. Eric got so silly on Emperor's Choice Tea that he was throwing napkin balls at a waitress. His aura is very healing and makes me feel grounded. He is so involved emotionally and politically – I really admire him – I feel like I could go off with him to fight like Diane Keaton did with Warren Beatty in "Reds," he's such a moving force. He does move me in my heart! Christmas came and went – I spent it as a true child of God, releasing my spirit to incredible heights. Height was where it was at yesterday, for Eric and I hiked for about 12 miles up to the top of a canyon. The enjoyment I had was so intense, I just kept experiencing power and peace at the same time – such centeredness – feeling like I was a strong Japanese woman with a pack on my back, walking in small even steps, my mind at tranquility's peak. We sighed a lot and moaned for joy. Wonder of wonders. Any time we hiked we would always feel sad coming off the mountain. Eric encouraged me to walk in front of him for part of the trail so I could be imbued with fairy energy; he claimed that whomever they touched first got the best "dose." *How good it feels to look into his eyes, to hear him tell me how good he feels with me, that he's warmer to other people after being with me – looking into him is like looking far away, looking beyond, into a gorgeous jewel.*

THE FIGHT TO END THE FIGHT

Eric was a political warrior completely engaged in "the cause." During this period in the early 1980's he was deeply concerned with the plight of Central Americans. The nations of Honduras, Nicaragua, El Salvador and Guatemala were undergoing U.S. invasions and experiencing vicious civil wars. Archbishop Romero and other Catholic clergy (nuns!) were gunned down. Eric's ardor penetrated everything; he could barely sleep sometimes, so caught up in the work he needed to do. I witnessed his being very upset one night, as he claimed he could hear the cries of the innocents for whom he struggled. He wrote letter after letter to government officials and he protested in front of our State Representative's office. Eric got arrested in San Francisco during the blockade of a port that shipped arms to El Salvador. He vehemently opposed our country's provision of weapons to another country whose corrupt army killed its nation's rebels.

Seeking to bring greater awareness to our area about the issue, Eric helped establish the local chapter of the Campaign for Peace with Justice in Central America (CPJCA). I had been vaguely aware of the turmoil in Central America but was now exposed to an alarming plight that appealed to my morality. It was like I was suddenly being slapped awake as I opened my eyes to the wicked injustice and deplorable cruelty. My heart directed me to take action in hopes of creating loud protest against the war in which the U.S. was participating. Besides, war and torture were two things I adamantly refused to accept as being tolerable, for I felt that humans should ultimately be more respectful of each other. (You're thinking, "How naïve," and I don't blame you. We love doing battle and I suspect we will continue in this fashion a few more centuries.) I assisted Eric in putting the CPJCA chapter together—we held weekly meetings, staged marches and vigils, set up a phone tree regarding any special bills presented to Congress, facilitated workshops, and protested by the freeway every Friday afternoon. I held my signs with great conviction, hoping to alert others about the ongoing atrocities, and believe me, the crimes were grotesque. Gravely, I wrote, *I was devastated after reading about some of the torture and beheadings in El Salvador – it was so terribly gruesome and obscene, I just couldn't find an answer to "why?" and that hurt. It is painful to face the horror that really exists – I'm troubled deep down. It burns up a lot of joy...I read about Guatemala and it changed my life. I feel more somber, more disturbed, and yet more activated, more willing to commit myself to The Work.*

Strife seemed to be all over the globe. Hindu tribesmen massacred one-thousand people in India, mostly women and children. My heart ached at the thought of humanity being so engulfed by darkness.

When Eric and I weren't working for justice in addition to our regular jobs, we continued to retreat into the mountains where it was safe to relax. It was our custom to bring along a baggie of raw almonds and a few oranges. One afternoon bees stung me ten times, but still I wrote, *After hiking eight hours it was as if a veil had been removed from my eyes – as if I'd had the best facial – as if I'd danced to my favorite music for a long time. I felt a kind of freedom that knew not the boundaries of my body or personality. It's funny how, when you expend energy thru the muscles, a new type of power comes in.*

The excitement of mountain topwind, and the joy of passing thru ever-changing terrain, all so wonderfully different, made for a remarkable day. I drew comfort from the steadiness of the stream.

Behold
God made this little flower
So simple, so intricate
Mandalas everywhere

Another place Eric and I frequented was the laundromat, and it was often here that we delved into the deep questions of life. *We did laundry together last night and were so involved in a discussion that we* didn't see that someone had stolen all of my underwear! Eric didn't do it! It's great that the laundromat has become a place of contemplation and journaling. Writing makes me feel indeed a lot clearer.

The reader may recall that Peter had been my first asexual boyfriend. I was originally going to label Eric as Number Two, but decided that it would be unfair to call him that. He might have been too overwhelmed by his calling to want to give himself to a serious relationship. He may have felt too guilty to allow himself pleasure more than a few times. Unfortunately, I was so in love with the young man that I wanted to physically unite with him **often**. I wrote, It was magical from the moment he walked in the door. Fire in the fireplace, fire in the bodies in front of it... I suspect there's more ground to cover in order for him to let me in deeper...We had a sexuality conflict (again) – I get down on myself for seeking that renewal, that recharge, that spirit contact. For him loverhood gets too demanding. I ought not to feel a bit silly for being a romantic - it's a play of the spirit...He said he'd marry someone right off who was doing just what he was. I'd like to catch up to him but I must follow the spirit at my own pace.

I asked Eric if he'd been unhappy and he said, "I just naturally am." Perhaps his deep solemnity is one thing that keeps us apart. I sadly think our exceptional relationship is closing its wings a bit - time will tell.

Eric left at midnight to go write letters to our officials. It's easy for him to shut off when it gets down to feelings, and immediately cast his attention on the world and its problems. I liked it a lot when we were not only political friends but also buddies beyond the Fight. Now I know what he meant when he said he could be very dry. Eric had a gentle airy voice but it got hard as rock when he felt pressure to do everything. I thought, "Lower your shield, Knight of Shining Ardor, your flame of purpose burns cold."

I wanted more of him than he could give. He had to cut me off. After all, I assumed the victims of terrible injustice were more important than his friendships. I felt great pain as Eric unraveled my connection with him. One night as we prepared to go to bed, he gave me an earnest look and spoke hesitantly. "I think...what it comes down to is that you and I are on different rays." A ray is considered one of seven planes of spirit-matter. Very esoteric. I froze. Shock sucked the air out of my lungs. Even though he was letting me go in a soft, indirect way, his judgment wounded me severely. Our relationship was now condemned. The safety dome that had formed around my heart from loving him was shattered, pieces of it stabbing at my vulnerable heart underneath its edges. Regardless of whatever trickery I could muster, I saw there was no chance we would stay together. All my charms could not compete with the polarization that he felt separated us. I just let it be. *I need to focus more of my efforts on work to be done and away from pleasure and memories of the love we shared, and let nature take its course with our current paths. I think it's probably the strength of his spirit, its fervor, that I am attracted to – part of me respects it for its exclusion of other things – it makes life easier, not having to deal with others as intensely – but I don't choose that path overall.*

In the mean time, my former boyfriend Peter was deathly ill. I went to visit him with homemade soup and he was throwing up blood. Upon being admitted to the hospital he was diagnosed with Good Pasteurs Disease, a rare illness in which part of the body eats away at another part. He needed plasma treatments for ten days. Eric and I brought him our sympathy and a big stuffed animal, and I was thrilled to hear that Peter's mother was concerned about him.

Eric decided to collect medical supplies to take to Nicaragua, joining the "Santa Barbara Eight" who visited the conflicted country as "peace ambassadors." Upon returning home the dear fellow brought back a case of hepatitis and trench foot, but assumed he had malaria. All he could do was lie around looking like a miserable puppy. His eyes were bright yellow in the corners. Initially he was told that he would need six months for his liver to improve, yet it was actually years before he felt much better. I positively hated feeling helpless at not being able to make him better. Maybe I thought that if I could care for him, he would take me back, but Eric ended up moving away to his mother's home to recover.

SAD STATISTICS FROM THE 1980'S

Notes taken from the remarks of a Santa Barbara photographer who
presented his slideshow on Central America

====

1000 kids died each day of malnutrition in Mexico, and
for a population of 70 million people, 50% were less than 15 years old!
Over 30 thousand refugees were in Honduras from El Salvador.
In El Salvador, 2% owned 60% of the land.
In Chiapas, Mexico 400 kids per month starved
in refugee camps.

As Eric was definitely too sick to continue "organizing," I took
on his leadership role. So much still had to be done from our little
corner of the world. While handing out leaflets downtown, I watched
women striding by in fancy clothes, women who looked like they
enjoyed pampering themselves. Although I admired their elegant
beauty, I compared them to the women refugees and victims trapped
in the world of war and brutality. The Americans with their gorgeous
hair, nails, makeup and expensive shoes disturbed me because they
symbolized the inequality and injustice that made life seem so
unbalanced. Some women decided what color to paint their nails, yet
other women watched family members die. Commenting about my
political activism I wrote, *I PRAY WITH ALL MY HEART that waves of
the will-to-good sweep across our body of government and that the
tide of torture turns. I see hope for social change – the World Peace
Tax Fund being considered, the Pope touring Central America... I did
more research on Guatemala and my sorrow keeps deepening, and I'm
confused about why I'm working with computers instead of poor
people. I had to get some sobbing and screaming out. My friend Sal,
the ceramist from El Salvador, has had relatives murdered. I would
almost be happy to go to jail for 6 months if I could keep a refugee
protected from the death squads.*

Dedicated to fellow activists:

Feeling about to break
under the mounting pressure
of holding up the torch
while fanning the light within
(hearing the cries of innocent victims)
struggling to make a step that can stop it
I despair over those who don't despair

I decided it'd be much better if I concentrated on the work I need to do instead of daydream about someone to share my passion with. Sometimes I feel like punishing myself for wanting things, but a good close friend might also take time away from The Work. I wonder if I am made of the kind of spirit that will lead me to work in Central America, or to really give of my whole body and personality and will – I'm such a mild radical.

Dear Lord! I am so confused! Part of me wants to retreat, a little, away from the meetings and organizing and hopelessness and frustration – but the other part knows it can't hide or turn away from the reality that there is so much to do, that the sacrifice must be made – the sadness can be overwhelming at times. I want so badly for there to be progress and I feel helpless in the sense that our actions aren't loud enough. The lonely part of me sometimes fights the politician in me – it wants time with a friend, time to be at leisure, time to be in love! But I suppose that because I haven't had such a person delivered yet that it's obvious I better get to work. Still, I must remember to refresh my spirit just like I do my body with vitamins.

During this hectic time of volunteering for the cause of justice, one of my favorite escapes was being in nature. Being in the woods renewed me and its fragrances acted as a tranquilizing balm. (My husband and kids always tease me about how much I enjoy my smelling faculty. Perhaps growing up around cigarette smoke as a kid or smoking pot as a young adult gave me a heightened appreciation for fresh air and pleasant scents.) Hiking and admiring the flowers on the trails were always good medicine. *I had to be among the plant kingdom -- it felt so good to feel like a child and giggle from happiness. Being outdoors made me much more susceptible to divine messages, as more TRUTH could be learned here. Dear me, the spectacles I witnessed [waterfalls, pools] – I felt such a deep gratitude for this day of nature exploration.*

At Grant Forest in the Sequoias, what glee I felt walking thru such serene land – there was a sweet mist for most of the day. It was Perfect, Divine Treasure. I felt slowed down, comforted that there IS such a beautiful world out there. Now I have added love and strength to use.

Bumblebees and ladybugs, in you
I find my quietness

Writing gave me sanctuary too. It helped me sort out my feelings and allowed me a safe place to express rage and grief. The suffering in the world and the urgency with which I wanted to alleviate it felt oppressive at times. I elaborated, *In a slide show on El Salvador, the aging in the children's faces was shocking. Boys of eleven looked seventeen – there was such seriousness in the eyes of five-year-olds. I just want to shut off my mind and have another reality take over. El Salvador has the most insecticide per acre of any nation in the world. Women suffocate their crying babies when hiding from the army. When I saw the film "El Norte" I cried the whole way through. I DEEPLY felt the suffering, and the inspiration to serve. I HAVE to do work that helps people, and not just in my free time. The movie made it so my heart will never be the same. If I want the world to be a better place to live, I could do so many things; I must decide what feels most important.*

I had seen a film on Grenada and then had a nightmare that night. The image of the woman with her backside blown open with organs exposed will stay in my head and make me question the perplexities of human nature for days to come.

I'm back to feeling that it's very hard to live in the world – but as I was biking home from work today, I realized that as there is a balance between the smell of car exhaust with the smell of flowers and lawns, so is there balance in what I see and what is.

A month of hard organizing is over. I'm making more room for enjoyment, but it's hard to feel okay doing so when the world is where it is. We raised over $1000 to help feed Guatemalan refugees.

The Fight was getting to be too much—too depressing, too frustrating and too much work. Not only was my phone being tapped but I had also become disillusioned about people in general. It seemed that there were always a few committed folks at the core who did most of the work and a whole lot of flaky unproductive ones on the edges. *After such a volatile meeting like the one tonight, I come away with the feeling that I don't trust politics, I don't understand them, I don't want to take a political side – I just need for my focus to be on human rights.*

I will always be fascinated by our species – such motivation to drive native peoples out. I WANT EVOLUTION FOR MANKIND!

Meeting after meeting: blah blah blob blob. I am getting sick of so much yak and hard work and defeat and organizing BLEH! My interest level in politics has dropped considerably, having read Illusions.

I've been trying to whip up a crowd to go to Sunday's march – I have become so cynical! I want to rely on someone else to be active for a change. Part of me really needs to fade out of activism and explore other parts of life, to be happier and not look at so much darkness – and another side of me wonders if maybe I would really be best off down in Mexico somewhere feeding people. UGH. So now I see myself being quite susceptible to cookie binges and depression and wishing I knew NEW people. I haven't even cared to look at the inside of a newspaper in 2 weeks. Dear world, please grow up. I need more laughing in my life.

A candle can only burn for so long; I eventually yielded to burnout. I allowed myself to turn away from the violence and bring my attention back to my needs. As one might expect, my thoughts returned to those of relaxation, fun and romance. Eric was up and around again and his pull on me hadn't diminished. His spirit was more bubbly and he flamboyantly flirted with me. I admitted, *Seeing Eric again, two hours seemed like ten minutes. Gosh how I still am wild about him, it's such a pain! Oh, how I could embrace him for hours. I can look at him and feel removed from him and/or feel like we are loving friends – but when we hug, it's another planet. Wish I had more time with Eric but he will probably always be a butterfly that will never land. He is such a nut though; he brought me a wrench and a cherimoya for Christmas!*

I am definitely still adjusting to sitting around a bit more. *I'm not sure how comfortable I feel when there is so much to be done for peace. However, right now I'm feeling somewhat vulnerable and had better not overextend myself. I have to remember the wisdom of that argument.*

*I saw the great value of taking time today – walking on the beach alone in the sun. I miss meditating – I'm beginning to under-stand how it **is** an act of service when I direct my thoughts to the right place.*

I granted myself the emotional room for self-pleasure slowly, as I easily found things to feel guilty about. Having been dubbed "the heart and soul of the Campaign" and then choosing to drop the ball felt traitorous. Eric would undoubtedly think less of me. Still, we were only friends now and I didn't need to try to impress him anymore. Re-nouncing the cause was a major adjustment and it was a painstaking process to let go of my control of the group. *In the evenings I wander about wondering what I should-could-be doing. God how I seem to be so dry of affection, wondering if I am escaping or searching. I came home and danced and tried to get clear on my shaky feelings of abandon and want.*

I've been picking at my fingers much more noticeably – I have less control over myself, not only in the physical realm but also in dreams, where Eric pops up with frequency. I feel ashamed and wish I wouldn't let myself be so haunted.

BOY CHASING AGAIN

Little did I know that the universe had a surprise in store for me. I arranged to carpool to a protest march at a nearby nuclear power plant with my friend Yank. He was bringing his housemate along. I went to Yank's house, and while waiting to leave I spied someone washing dishes in the kitchen. The band of light surrounding the young man intrigued me. It later occurred to me that that moment was one of those incredible experiences when serendipity creates that tingly feeling. It turned out that the guy at the sink was the same person I danced with the night before at my last hurrah/fundraising event. Having raised more money for Guatemalan refugees felt very satisfying, but the big bonus was getting to flit about the friendly and handsome creature called Jake. He was thin, muscular, soft-spoken and had an olive complexion. Though his teeth had a few small gaps, he had a nice smile and full lips. I was drawn to his charming face like children are to kittens and puppies.

I could tell Jake was sweet but it was also obvious that he was silly. He told dumb jokes on the car ride and kidded around exces-sively. I preferred looking at him rather than listening to him! On the protest march, however, we learned that we were both vegetarians and that similarity formed an instant bond between us. (Over the years we would find that despite living in California, most restaurants had little vegetarian food to offer.) Back at his house we politely said our goodbyes, and I left feeling unsure about my status as potential romantic material. My quick judgment of his goofiness, however, was overridden by my attraction to him. I figured I'd give him a second chance if he called me. We could at least go out for health food together. The problem was, I waited for that call for two weeks! I finally asked Yank if Jake was interested in me. (Red flag! Jake's lack of commitment would interminably plague our relationship.)

I had wanted fun back in my life and got it. Jake did want to date me. He had enchanting stories to tell about his college days abroad in Kenya and about his family of eight siblings. We dined, danced, rode bikes and hiked, but what particularly appealed to me was his skill at shoulder and neck massage. He had good strong hands from carpentry, and this type of work also helped fit him with a virile body, like that of a Greek god or a model. Additionally, he possessed that hardy sense of humor, the style of which I was warming up to. Overall we were a nicely matched couple, but I still harbored some reservations about giving myself completely to him. I wasn't the best judge of character and he could have had only one thing on his mind. *I hope he turns out to be sincere – not just out for "the challenge." I fear that his objectivity (more head than heart) will prove to be a recurring pattern of boyfriends that don't give fully or are confused too much to really pay attention. Jake is awfully good at being calm and cheerful but not so good at knowing if he's feeling something, if he is!*

The first time we kissed our teeth banged together. The second time was pure bliss. I began to think of little else other than Jake. As it can often be in new relationships, our lovemaking some-times took hours. (After many years of marriage, we efficiently got it down to five minutes.) We had only been dating a few months when my housemate needed to move, and as I needed someone else to help pay the rent, Jake signed on as live-in lover. (What the heck, I kept a cleaner house than he and Yank did.) I didn't pay much attention to Red Flag #2: the longest relationship he had had was four months. I was too mesmerized by his affections, his handsomeness and his handiness. He could fix anything. His work was always high quality craftsmanship. I told him, "Jake, you are the best carpenter since Jesus." Pumping him up couldn't hurt.

"Riiiiiiiight." He looked at me skeptically.

Lord, to be in love with an angel in the spring is heaven on earth. How big my heart is for him. It seemed I had closed up a lot of myself doing political work – the joy was so rare, as was the peace from calmness, or thinking that was not clouded with pictures of death and war...

It's hard to find inner quietness when the mind dreams of love and its many images. I feel less drawn toward my own interests and more toward being in his arms...Lately I've been ragging on myself for the amount of wasted energy I spend thinking about "settling down," especially when I'm reminded from old diaries of my propensity for being "wifey." Jake's not very close with his family; could he be a family man at all?

As both love and its corresponding fear became more intense for us, Jake shied away from strong emotions. I determined that he was either a shallow person or that he refused to let me penetrate the locks around his heart. I complained, *I kidded him about how good it is to "play house" because you get a lot done, and he said, "Don't get any ideas." He rarely uses any imperatives so I felt it was a pretty strong thing to say. Jake had been moody and I got upset for his shutting me off. His friend remarked that he keeps a lot of emotion inside. Even so, he's the best man for telling me he loves me so often. That softens me incredibly.*

Feeling angry and discouraged, I would withdraw to the comfort of the outdoors. *Plants make me feel so comfortable, it's easy to feel friendship with them. Many times I like them more than I like people. The sun soothes me tremendously. Sitting here I feel like a babe being cradled. Being in this park is instant calm. My spirit clicks into the rhythm of the natural world here. I feel such a tremendous affinity with the buds, the rustling leaves, the enchantment of the plants and their colors – if only that power of closeness with nature would flow into other areas of my life...*

While my love boat with Jake was being rocked, Eric happened to weasel his way into my life once more. I wondered if Eric had sensed that he had a second opportunity to woo me and I wrote, *It's really funny but Eric seems to be acting closer to me now that Jake is around. Eric seems refreshed in one sense and also in just as much despair in another. I so admire that flame in him to serve humanity, to end the suffering. Sometimes I wonder how I can sit back and not take action.*

Jake brought me a big bouquet of roses for no apparent reason and then one night in our rapture he said, "Be mine" – hmm!

All I had needed was the confirmation that Jake truly wanted me. Perhaps it was my penchant for sentimentality, but I felt like I had hooked the best catch and was determined to reel it in. I was now absolutely certain that he was the one for me.

Thinking about our lovemaking last night I just melt upon thinking of the way his face looked, so full of that shared communion – he IS indeed that man I always fantasized about as a young girl, that gentle soul I longed to be near.

He thinks we'd be very happy being married and he doesn't rule it out, but it's just too soon. My heart is overly anxious at times. I don't know why I'm not satisfied with just living with him. I'm too attached to Jake, and thinking about marriage to anyone is fucked because of my jealousy and insecurity. I guess I really don't like the aspect of marriage because of the risk of pain involved – it's just the romance I like, which more than likely wouldn't last. Jake doesn't communicate enough, and I feel it's damaging to us. He thinks that thoughts and feelings are petty – doesn't that suggest his life is petty? Maybe Libras really aren't as deep as I thought.

The metronome of love was ticking back and forth between joy and pain. The world itself was certainly dishing out painful events during the mid-eighties. One alarming occurrence was the horrible murder of a young woman from our city. A man lured her under false pretenses into his car, took her up into the mountains and dismembered her. War continued in Central America. (The Contras were Nicaraguan soldiers conducting widespread brutality against their fellow countrymen suspected of supporting the Sandanistas. Our government was soon voting on giving the Contras military aid.) I lamented, *I'm having a very hard time reconciling my personal life with my view of the world – I see and feel so much that is very negative for the earth. With the vote for Contra aid coming up again I feel so emotional, like I am somehow responsible for those people in Central America. Yet even if I were to take more action, I don't believe it would help them really. I guess I'm angry at the forces causing all of this pain, in me and in them. I feel trapped by my wanting to assume some "fault" for the injustice, or for not helping in the struggle.*

I feel so crushed inside, my heart bleeds. Although I am taking *no major action towards the Contra aid, I feel so deeply about it and experience such great pain from it. I could be overreacting but GOD just to think that $27 million is going to them, when our social service agencies could use it – let alone the horror being played out on innocent peasants... 16 people were arrested at our Representative's office – great, but it doesn't go very far! I sure don't think it'd be that far-fetched an idea for me to kill myself in protest – that would say something! We've tried so hard for so long. I feel motionless inside, like I am completely thwarted.*

With the aid vote being such a serious and controversial topic, Eric created a radio program called "The Other Americas" to get the issues aired locally and nationally. He wanted different voices on his shows, so it was natural for him to ask me to help since I had those few years of disc jockey work behind me. Jake ended up volunteering, for he knew I couldn't commit to anything else political, and perhaps he didn't want me spending time with Eric. I confided, *I was feeling like I couldn't get involved again, especially because of my strange feelings about Eric. There's still an attraction that I can't stand. It does seem pretty peculiar that Eric and Jake are so similar in certain ways – carpenters, veggies, liberal and cute. I amuse myself by watching what my mind does around Eric. It flits right to him, his bright eyes...*

Reagan's been elected and I fear more Central America invasions. I wish I would let myself shut off the potential nightmares of what could go wrong so that I could try to live contentedly. I have free time which I could commit to some worthy cause – I'm back to feeling I need to help someone or some group – work environmentally – is it guilt or ego?

I'm feeling stress over the darkness I see in the world. How much responsibility should I take?

Another great fortune:
"The sun will always shine through your heart,
onto your smile,
and warm your soul."

LOVE IS A MANY SPLINTERED THING

Living with your lover before committing to marriage is a smart concept. I always liked "playing house" and Jake was a good candidate for the long-term. As a carpenter, he whipped up custom bookshelves and tables upon demand. He had great ideas for home improvements and was skilled in car maintenance. He was energetic and attentive. I enjoyed the process of making our rental house feel homey and began to think of myself as a novice yuppy. I had cultivated a reverence for adulthood, and found great satisfaction in rearranging the furniture. At twenty-six, it hadn't yet dawned on me that my maternal clock was starting to tick loudly.

You might think that a guy from a nice family with seven sisters (and a brother) wouldn't have any problems living with a woman. However, Jake started feeling too mothered. It even bothered him when I mentioned he had a shoelace untied. In turn, he bugged me by smacking his food, making sniffing noises and bringing lots of dirt into the house. We rode that roller coaster of love a lot, sometimes holding on tightly, and sometimes falling out. The real problem was, *Jake says he's scared of being with someone for a whole lifetime – it's such a reinforcement that it'll never happen with him. I would like to be the one for him but there's just no use trying to be someone different.*

I realized I must remember that my life here and now with Jake is quite wonderful and I really do seem to be spoiling it if I forget how good it is, all things considered.

Obviously my desires weren't meant to come true yet, so I should be working on other things, like my fixation with certain ideas! This bull can be a bully! Last night I was wishing that Jake would be more affectionate with me, especially after seeing friends hug and kiss so much. I discovered that perhaps I just want to feel in love again and have someone be in love with me – it does make the world so much more magical. How can I bring that out in him? I wonder if it's at all possible.

I realized that I've been feeling resentment because he's not ready to take me, and I feel guilty for wanting so much from him. I also discovered that I tend to rely on him for my entertainment, and that if on my own I will do a lot more.

I feel torn every day between one extreme and another. Part of me is seeking more playful times, getting around more, dreaming of knowing different men. The yin half wants to control that urge for flitting about and giving up too early, striving for the long-term goal. I resist the thought of leaving this situation but I know it's not really right.

Alas, it seemed like our destiny to be together wasn't panning out. He was too wishy-washy, noncommittal and afraid. Since he didn't have any burning desire to marry me, I took a firm stand and booted his butt out. He needed to find his own place, get his head out of the hole and get clear on his dreams. In the meantime I would wait, watch and see if anything changed. *He admitted to being in a quandary. The poor guy runs away from emotion – doesn't think it's spiritual. His mind is so active he doesn't settle down to his feelings. Jake hasn't really gotten much from our separation, he says, because he hasn't yet really faced what he needs to do. He says he doesn't want to lose me, but he doesn't make a great effort at preventing that either. I have feelings of fear and sadness when I think about what could happen – the picture breaking. I don't feel accepting of letting my dream go yet because I still have hope – but I'm not sure why. To be honest I don't think I'm gonna figure in much more of his life, per his choice. His needs are different enough that, when he does look at them, they are hindered terribly by mine. I am still such a silly dreamer – I fantasize of his sending me flowers, or begging me to come back to him. I live in a daydream half the time.*

It dawned on me one night in the bathtub---a key place where I let Spirit advise me---that I had to get on with my life and pursue other things besides husbands. Jake and I still dated a little but I empowered myself by joining a local gospel choir and also singing with the City College chorale. I wanted to be more lively and proactive

73

instead of waiting to be someone's wife, and felt that singing would open me up socially. I wanted to immerse myself more in the community, but without giving up my indulgence in private time. I had almost forgotten how much I relished that alone time, and wrote, *Today has been incredibly splendid. I feel so relaxed and accomplished and joyful. Took a stroll, cleaned out my closet and drawers, planted wildflower seeds, finished a cross-stitch project... There's something about the quality of the day, or maybe it's simply my frame of mind? As I watch the sky change colors I see it as my life picture - always transforming to deeper tones.*

I have so enjoyed going back in time and memory in my diary. So much has expanded in me. I'm thankful for writing. Even got a great book about "diaryism" – I feel deeply pleased to be part of that collective that loves doing this so much.

I had plenty to do but life still didn't feel complete. What it boiled down to was hormones. I realized I was ready for a family! Jake would throw out these little bits of bait that made me hopeful he was changing, as in, *Jake says he really misses living with me and still thinks we'll get back together.* Yet I could see Jake's pattern of hemming and hawing. He wove it tightly about him. His indecision was a cloak he wore to bind him safely away from the unknown. I tried to relax my grip on the man of my dreams and reported, *It's sad, not to feel like I can fully give of myself to Jake, so I feel partly detached from him. I wish he could receive all that I have to give. I thought today there IS someone out there who would love to be with me and make a family; I need to release Jake to allow more to happen. But then I miss him and wish I were more independent of him. The feeling of niceness when we're together doesn't match up with rightness.*

I knew I had to find support outside of the romantic conflict I was steeped in and found guidance from my wise women friends. "Sacred circle time" was a weekly spiritual space held at the home of a teacher/healer. The classes were offered to those seeking release, wanting to recharge, and commune with the Creator in their hearts. I found great benefit from sharing in this group setting, yet simultaneously resisted opening up my vault of feelings – the intense ones often being under "lockdown." *In the circle I still cover up the minutest things as if the truth would make me feel ashamed. I must still have a lot of fear - I don't take criticism well even at my age.*

Funny how I had asked to have an angel come to me for help and we did Angel Cards tonight in the circle. I was so heartened to see them. When we met our angels I saw how gorgeous they are, and truly felt the LOVE they have and the spirit of Him they pour out. What gratitude. Amazing to think they care so much about my little troubles. They were the Angels of Efficiency and Release. I need to be efficient at eliminating those old pictures! Release everyone else's ideas! Throw out those old patterns! I must turn off the chatter to hear Their Messages. Sometimes I feel I'm on the verge of opening up more, to acquainting God more fully, but I keep myself on the same level – fear. I get glimpses of a grander spiritual life and can see that there is so much more.

I've been really starting to deal with why I talk to myself at almost every opportunity – I think it may have to do with all the words I never spoke while I was growing up. Why must my lips echo my mind?

Taking the arduous path of personal growth meant that writing was vital for me and necessary for better health. There were moments when I felt like my soul was poking at my outer self, urging me to write, as if the act of writing down my thoughts and feelings would hasten my emotional balance.

My desire to learn more about what God had put in me suddenly grew more serious, and I began placing more focus on my higher self rather than the conflicts I was helping to create. I felt that the "Great Mystery" led me to visit a co-worker who had a book on her coffee table that instantly attracted me, its strong energy calling out to me. I picked up <u>A Course in Miracles</u> and knew I had no choice but to read it. Its text and workbook lessons were invaluable guides that helped me obtain inner peace and they saved me incalculable times— from harm, from fear, and from myself. I documented some reasons for needing spiritual nourishment and mental discipline in the following excerpts: *I have been feeling in the throes of chosen emotional turmoil and am back to resorting to ice cream for fulfillment. Guilt is too often all pervasive. I'm afraid of going to the healing circle because of my fear of having a lot of attention when I feel sad and dark, and I'm embarrassed by my emotion. Right now I'm half writing and half picking off my nail polish.*

Miracle-mindedness also helped me tackle my male interactions while I remained romantically topsy-turvy. Jake and I were still going out, but nothing was resolved. I was hanging on half-heartedly. I wrote, *I think I've been seeing Jake too much – I don't want to feel too hooked in again. He's a darling man but too confused! He asked, "Why can't we have a nice non-descriptive relationship?"*

It's AMAZING what just happened. Eric called me at work so I met him at the co-op. He seemed really happy to be with me. We went out to eat and then came home because he said he loved watching Jeopardy. Hmm! After sitting and just being together, he hugged and kissed me and "threw" me on my bed! I felt open to him, like it was nice and natural to be lying beside him, but I didn't allow my heart to open up totally – I wasn't passionate in a physical sense. He sure was, and easily could've seduced me – but I made him catch his bus on time. Eric thought Jake and I were completely broken up, and it did make me feel happy to think he was sorta "waiting" for me to be available. Huh, I wonder! I also doubt it. He did say he read over his journals of when we were together and it had been a happy time for him. Still, he's such a cynical man. I think I'm over my worshipping the guy!

Weeks would go by where I felt like I didn't have solid footing beneath me. One day I would be slipping on Jake's emotional ice, and the next day he would affirm his love for me. Despite the occasional tender evenings we shared, the struggle to ascertain if our relationship would sink or swim just got to be too much. I was ready to start a new year off as truly single. *January 1, 1986. I'm sad and I'm a fool. I have "resolved" not to let myself see Jake except when absolutely necessary. Desire does lead to suffering – I'm playing such a game with myself. I see my pattern with men, turning them away if they* don't fall into what I want them to be. Happens every time. I waste their friendship. Now I don't even let Jake kiss me. I feel cold and don't like myself for being so stingy with my affection. I don't like how I seem to want him to feel bad.

Last night I dreamt I had a baby girl, I was arrested, I was engaged, and someone I know died, all in three different dreams! Jake dreamt he was to act as a king in a play and he didn't know his lines at all – how symbolic! I find refuge in the idea that I don't want to marry someone without goals anyway. Shit! I want to free myself of all this energy that tires me – I've been dwelling in it since last summer – but it seems like in order to let it go I must not see him.

So glad I dreamt last night of having a new romantic interest – it's fun to remember how it feels, first getting to know someone when anything can happen. It's very bizarre for me lately, how part of me will feel sad and sensitive and negative about me and Jake, and the other part could care less and is more interested in meeting a new man. I hear my rational mind whispering a lot, even while my "emotional mind" whimpers and knows it's being silly. Still, I feel ill – releasing involves the whole body. I could sleep so easily, to escape.

My romantic struggle with Jake put me in the doldrums. I knew I needed an extra dose of inspiration and decided to catch a sunrise down at the harbor. It wasn't a long bike ride from home and I wrote, *I have so enjoyed watching everything – the fishing boats sssnnnaaaiiiling out to sea, the waves hurtling the breakwater, the opal colors in the sand, the clouds as they do their chameleon dance...*

Another primo spot I loved was the Santa Barbara Botanic Garden and it was one of my favorites. I took great pleasure in scouting out the perfect spots for writing and contemplating (there were many) and I observed, *Dear God, the glory of Your creation makes my heart glad. Smelling the renewed vigor of the earth after 2 days of rain is ecstasy. Even greater that that is admiring Your many thoughts of petals and colors and designs of spring.*

◆ ◆ ◆ ◆ ◆ ◆ ◆

INTERLUDE

I love how days in the spring are always different – the clouds and the landscape offer unique pictures of beauty. Living by the hills and the bay gives me an array of climate pockets. Today's colors are muted and the estuary is smooth and grey. Tomorrow it will be a shimmery cobalt, offset nicely by the bright green of the foothills. Admiring the greenness after a good rain I think, "Children, do you see what I see? I see utter joy." I so wish that I could capture these profound moments of ecstasy and give them to the kids. Yet, this view may not sing to them. All I can hope is that they find the gift of sublime resonance in other simple things.

◆ ◆ ◆ ◆ ◆ ◆ ◆

Santa Barbara was a town with loads of character but it also had earthquakes, and I recorded, *Right at 7:30 am as I was going for the door to work, wham! What a loud rumble. The dishes were rattling and a bowl fell on the floor. My heart was pounding as I stood in the doorway, waiting for the worst to come at any second. I wondered, should I stay here? How long will this last? Will it be safe to ride my bike to work? It measured 4.5 but felt bigger. So weird to feel the whole house shake and wobble under my feet. And I told myself, "Yep, this is why I always thought it was foolish to live in California!*" (Subsequent shakers like the one in Northridge, California were much scarier, but thankfully I have never experienced having my television fly across the room.)

Further upsets with Jake continued to shake up my world as well. He mentioned that he had been about to propose but had had a psychic reading that convinced him we should definitely split up. I griped, *I felt like calling Jake and telling him what a fool and a creep he is – but that's just emotional release garbage. It's funny to listen to the thoughts in my head lately like, "I'll show him" and "Boy did he blow it!" After I resolved it was over he called me at work – he's definitely a hard one to be finished with.* But Jake had enough sense to get a counselor's viewpoint. I was encouraged to hear that he had strong emotions after a few sessions and appeared to be moving through some issues. He was opening up to love more. *For Valentine's Day he had left me a basket of red tulips at work, along with some balloons, streamers, coffee chocolates, and fifteen candles at home in my room. I am amazed at how much good sex opens up the chakras [energy centers]. I felt like I wanted to keep Jake near me all day. His beauty is at times overwhelming.*

"If you learn nothing else in life, learn to love yourself." Joseph

The women's sacred circle that I had been attending was now a weekly healing class for men as well. The group gave me the nickname "Birdy" because of my quick nervous movements and love of singing. Learning took place on many levels. The participants were all teachers for each other, but a few could "channel" communications from the spirit realm. Steve claimed to have channeled the message above from Joseph, Mary's husband. I was astounded by how high the energy felt that I did not doubt the authenticity of the experience; love's presence was so powerful I believed the group was truly receiving a statement of wisdom from the divine.

Several of the people in the class seemed to have some real problems -- nothing terribly traumatic, just deep-seated fears that were good fuel for the communal fire. One single mom had awful arguments with her teenage son, and another struggled with grief at losing her mother. Everyone was given safe space in which to purge their troubles with the group's loving support. In class I brought my childish brain patterns into clearer focus and turned them over to God, gaining valuable insight along the way. Admittedly, these comments sound like déjà vu. I have embarrassed myself at "taking so long" to recover from my poor self-esteem and having to repeat my lessons over and over. The big one that I do need to hear regularly is that I make a choice, every minute, in how I see things. *Indeed I've shrugged away, or even thrown off, compliments from people. I have a pattern of not wanting attention and whisking it right off me. Weird! Like I didn't want to feel good. And why don't I like feeling or appearing weak? Part of me sees how lovely I am inside but the other part attacks everything.*

I was feeling nervous, upset and confused about the world and my responsibility for caring for others' suffering. In healing group I got the message, "Sweet little Birdy, fly free. You don't need to toil so hard on the earth. Take the image of the sparrow into your heart." It's still tough to balance out giving and receiving and deserving, but I feel more in tune with the harmony of such a balance. One of my teachers said I was afraid of having it all – marriage, bliss, etc.

Today I allowed myself to feel the rebirth I was wanting. Oh blessed day, my heart almost hurt from the joy and expectancy and love for myself that I needed to help me grow. I shared that it was like "little Birdy is drinking rainbow juice," the way I feel so nourished by the Light and by the love in the group.

Having many journals to review gave me renewed understanding time and time again. Returning to those old diaries gave me answers to questions I hadn't considered asking before. Rereading passages helped me dig deeper and move through some blocks I faced in my group sessions. Years ago and still today, I read entries that reveal layers of my personality that I had buried. I uncover patterns that cry out for change. I see those places where I was too slow to act, and hear the words I should have said. In the end, I love every bit—every failure, guilt trip and disappointment. They have sculpted and defined my uniqueness.

If only I had consistently meditated since the time I started to in college --- I might have gone far in wisdom.

I had visions of going through a gate and meeting the Angel of

Trust. He was dressed in flowing white robes and his arms were outstretched. He led me around, deeper, and then we danced a number of steps, the planet below us. I felt carefree and detached from the earth. Then he held me, as it was when I was first learning to swim, his hand under my back, and we floated down to earth. To allow him to stay with me, I pictured his arm around my shoulder, never leaving – he was always inside too. He's not something I can really force, he just is. I feel like maybe I've earned him. He is essential for my growth. He is the opposite of fear, and being fearful feels more and more distant to me. I am learning how much POWER there is in not being fearful.

One morning I was really feeling the effects of drinking 2 nights in a row. My guilt gradually increased, even though it was a strictly mental process I could observe. By late afternoon I had allowed a high fever to attack me that gave me chills too. My voice got real hoarse. I looked up the meaning of these symptoms in Heal Your Body and it said anger, burning up. I didn't quite feel anger, although I was upset with myself. I worked on still loving myself and forgiving me my passions. As I relaxed in bed I used all the powers I knew to heal myself and pulled the heat out of my aura. I asked myself what was wrong – and after searching for the meaning within, I was given a steady inflow of messages – I was going through a purification. God wants me to be more pure. I need to turn within for the highs. As I was in a state of deep relaxation I heard so MUCH, especially after singing the gospel songs in my head, focusing on Jesus and the power of the Light. I had the thought that maybe I had toxic shock and could die, but repeated to myself that I wasn't afraid. I knew I'd be healed in the morning. I woke up at 12:30 am and felt cool, and felt a miracle had happened. I told myself not to worry, and so, there wasn't anything to actually worry about!

We now return to my love story with Jake that twists and turns. You, faithful reader, could easily have concluded that we should have been done with each other, but despite the odds, we still had more awkward growing to do as a pair. The universe was undeniably keeping us united as an on-again, off-again couple. I was thinking how

I don't trust Jake, or myself when I'm with him – I need to unstick my-self from all the gummy expectations and old feelings. He continues to want me for his girlfriend. I wish I would release my expectations and he would release his fear. I feel guilty because marriage seems to come out of possessiveness. I'm bugged because Jake kept saying how much he loves me and doesn't want to be without me, but he has no follow-through! He spoke of his increased sexual desire, due to hav-ing lived with me, and of his interest in other women. I suppose that's one reason he can't accept marriage yet.

It's so odd how I flip-flop about how I feel about Jake, but right now I'm feeling like I'm ready to call it a good game and find a new player.

I went to tell Jake my honest feelings about us and he said he had been dreading the conversation. Right away his whole body started shaking from the fear – it caught me aback, the emotion was so strong. He said he didn't want me to completely "snuff the light out" or to "uproot the plant" – that if I were going to ditch him entirely he'd probably leave town – that he was honored I considered spending the rest of my life with him. I said I could no longer live on hope, the rela-tionship wasn't serving me anymore, that still holding onto me he was being closed to other people – he agreed that we should take a vaca-tion from each other, and have no contact until my birthday.

Jake and I had not seen each other for 3 weeks so we could be clear. On our reunion he brought me a bouquet of sweet peas. Throughout the day I'd get a heart flutter thinking about him. I noticed quite a change in him physically – all that digging at work had really expanded his chest – wow! I was hooked! He said to have faith in him. All in all I feel love flowing greatly with Jake.

It was quite a surprise when early one evening I heard Jake playing the guitar outside my window. He rarely played, and here he was playing Elton John's "Your Song" and singing! It sounded really good! When he came in and we hugged, there was a lump in his sweatshirt, and I detected a ring box immediately but couldn't believe it was possible.

We went to the beach and sat on a picnic table. Night had

fallen and the waves pounded the shore. Jake was being goofy. I told him to speak up since the surf was so loud. I glanced at the stars and wondered if tonight was the night. He joked, "Will you m-m-m-marinate my steak for me?"

"What?"

"Will you m-m-make me a martini?"

"Ummm...."

"Miss Lilibella, will you marry me?"

"Okay. Yes!" Again I looked up at the sky and thanked my lucky stars. I never thought he would ask. We hugged and hugged. *I suggested that he not take more than three weeks to see if he had to back out, and he said all right but that he wouldn't.* (What was I thinking?)

My dearest friend Julie was proposed to at least a dozen times. This first time for me was a big deal. Jake had popped the question the night before Julie and I were flying to Hawaii for a fun getaway. We made great travel buddies and laughed a lot. (If anyone should write a book, Julie should – that girl always had the most incredible stories, and her memory was so sharp she could pinpoint the date of just about anything I asked. She went to high school with comedian Tim Allen—did you know that his real name is Tim Dick?) The trip was dreamy for me as I relished the events of Jake's proposal and went over them many times in my head. Being proposed to was a huge relief and the culmination of so many struggles. Now I could relax and let all those romantic notions flourish in my imagination. *Before I go to sleep I like to visualize him and dream about our future – what happiness I feel to be able to let myself float into the joy.*

Not long after my return from vacation, Jake attended a "Heart Seminar" which was a program designed to help people open to love. Regardless of being engaged, he admitted that he had done a little flirting. I huffily took the ring off but he insisted that I *wear the ring and feel it. He confided that he's afraid of not having his freedom and committing to an unknown, and not being comfortable with having so much love because he was used to being the lonely boy.*

Into that unknown we went together. I found a gorgeous used

wedding dress in the newspaper and it fit nicely to my shape. I prided myself on being thrifty. My mom got quite perturbed that I hadn't let her see it first; it was such a good deal that I snatched it without hesitation. Shortly thereafter it was on Mom's fiftieth birthday that I discovered I was pregnant. Supposedly the diaphragm had failed. "Oh my God Kalila, no! What are you going to do?"

"It really is terrible. I can't believe it. We don't know yet." I held Jake's hand tightly. He was pale and reserved.

Being pregnant has been an interesting experience – being tremendously constipated, feeling exhausted all the time, having crappy hangover symptoms in the morning, having abnormal eating patterns, and getting huge boobs!

I refused to be pregnant before being married. It was so backwards and it wasn't the right time for that stage yet. To my way of thinking back then, babies should come after weddings, and I was firmly sticking to that picture. I wanted to get married because a man adored me and not because a baby was making me get hitched. I worried that a child this soon would put undue stress on our relationship. It was a horrific choice to make and I felt terrible about going through with it, but I ended up picking the abortion. I acknowledged, *Here I am, waiting for the future to be the past. Last night I was up crying, being afraid and feeling terrible. I hate the word abortion. I never thought I'd have one in my karma – that I would have to hide it in my past.* I was sick with myself and mad as hell about the diaphragm, but I wanted a husband first. I wanted to start our marriage off in the old-fashioned, "proper" way. It was simply awful walking in and out of the abortion clinic, yet how fortunate I was not to meet up with any protesters; I was able to slink home in shame without having to fight off the pro-lifers.

It wasn't until the formal wedding invitations arrived in the mail that Jake decided to abort too. It hurt so much to see his face drop when he saw the announcements in fancy print, as if he'd just lost a big hand at a casino, or that as a pirate he had just been given the "black spot." I wanted to say, "Hon, we really are getting married, right?" Apparently he was okay with just the idea of marriage and not the reality, but I had been under the impression that the ring meant he was ready. Clearly I had to let him go. Again. *I'm amazed how strong I can be when it seems my beautiful world is falling apart. Maybe it's just that I don't want to feel the pain. Yet when I tried to scream into my pillow, a little cry came out and then a laugh. It's hard to be angry at someone I love so much and also pity and understand. On the other hand I don't think I know him well – it's as if he's playing a game.*

PLUNDER AND SPLIT ASUNDER

Jake agreed that before we officially broke off the engagement, he would first explore more deeply his fear of getting married. We met an MFCC counselor who shed a light on our plight. *Apparently Jake is living in the future too much, thus creating for himself a lot of anxiety. He also uses a lot of childish words – indecisive words – kind of, sort of, I guess, maybe. Our system of my hurriedness and his hesitancy doesn't make for a good start – it's great he loves himself and me enough to probe into his confusion. If in the next month we realize marriage isn't right for him, then I can better accept it knowing exactly why. He feels so ashamed of what's happened, but how fantastic it is that the conflict has been uplifted to the point that he will be healed through it. I can now see beyond his "immaturity."*

Jake wasn't the only one having problems with the marriage dilemma. My mom couldn't bear seeing the wedding postponed. She could not accept the fact that Jake was emotionally unprepared for it, and she was distraught with disappointment. It hurt her too much to see her kid being let down. In defending Jake, I bore the brunt of her bitterness. She was throwing acrid seasoning into the stew of my life and I didn't like the taste. *Mom is being so bitter and judgmental about our postponing the wedding. Jake feels very badly about "shattering my dreams." She predicts we'll never get married. Sadly, her anger is suffocating my respect for her. She is critical / sarcastic and hard for me to deal honestly with. I just want to handle this myself and not have to try to get her approval.* Mom and I agreed to take a week long vacation from speaking to each other. She needed time to cool down. After our break she told me, "I'm going to be angry for a long time." I felt like saying, "Great! I'm sure that will do you a lot of good!" *She cancelled reservations at the resort already, removing herself from any part of the wedding plans. It'll almost be more of a mess if he decides to go through with it! Mom and I do not see eye to eye spiritually – she didn't understand about the Divine Plan, how we are all taken care of and we grow through what we choose – it does create more of a noticeable distance between us. I want another chance! She probably thinks I'm such a fool to stay with someone who botched things up.*

Still engaged, uncertain and yet hopeful that we wouldn't ultimately break up, Jake and I bought a funky old house together. The place needed a ton of work. It was a very affordable dive with a huge backyard in which Jake hoped to build a home he would design himself. I loved the blue bachelor buttons growing near the house and the two huge pine trees the wind whispered through. It took us many evenings to work our way around the house and make her insides sparkle with new paint and some modern fixtures. What a sensual job the painting was, stroking and caressing the bare wood all over the place. The renovation took so much time that I found I had done very little writing but plenty of decorating. Later we discovered how much we enjoyed buying older properties and transforming them into cute places with style and spiffy landscaping.

During the home makeover process, Jake continued to search his soul. He obviously needed to bolster the rocky foundation that the home of his heart rested upon, but he was taking too long. I vented, *I wish he knew what he's doing to me. I don't see when things are going to be stabilized. I feel so let down, like I can't get in the game because I'm too biased a referee. It's like going around Monopoly™ and getting the same cards over and over.*

Jake slept over two nights in a row and it was weird, both nights I had dreams of someone's throat being cut!! Ick, is that symbolism.....?

I broke off the engagement. Guess I didn't want to be open to hurt, so I took my power and dealt it. I feel like I've deserted him in a way, but I couldn't keep waiting. My golden egg of – patience? – cracked. I have to admit the incredibly deep disappointment I feel about everything, yet I seek to find the wisdom in the experience.

Lugging emotional distress weighed heavily on me. I wisely allowed the members of the healing group to support me as I limped along. I hated feeling vulnerable and needy, and *confessed to being tired of feeling defensive.* The relief that the group offered made me feel like I was in a typical orange juice or breakfast commercial, where a window with lovely curtains opened up and a ton of light flooded in. I was inspired to compose two bits of prose in gratitude for my spiritual buddy-helpers:

Honoring the Awakening
I take joy in seeing the mothering of our perfect selves
In the garden of awareness
We're becoming a field of fertile souls
Sprouting up in eager attention
Saluting the sun in our hearts

Glorious it is to be free, to arise...
And wonderful to wake to a new day
By the passionate poetry of
the Light calling

◆ ◆ ◆ ◆ ◆ ◆ ◆

i
little
did I know...?
crawling, stepping off
cliffs of clingy fear
twisted inside guilt

but then
led to Real-Eyes
how warm your blanket
how hot my heart
what joy breathing in
New Life

I
little did I know!
how huge am I in light!
leaping, flying over
peaks of dreamy wonder
witnessing the Glory

and always coming
to rest in that Place
the crystal altar of Truth
greeting Angels within
and beyond
how I marvel at Perfection
and laugh

Having been worried that he was taking too long and might lose me for good, one evening Jake took himself out to the back yard and sobbed. He cried at how lovely my garden was. He cried at what a struggle it had been for us. He wept at how horrible it would be for us not to share our days and nights together, and he let his fears pour out with his tears. The clarity that resulted from his wet face and open heart gave him the realization that he could be happily married to me. It seemed as if love suddenly gave him the green light that signaled "Yes! Step on it and go get the girl!" With big firm hugs I welcomed his earnest commitment, knowing that this was it; after many loops around the game board we had made it to the big glittery square of treasure at last. The following evening he placed several candles and vases of flowers all around our room, and hung up handmade posters expressing his love. Eight months to go until The Big Day.

Over the next several months Jake and I calmed down, settling into the routines of work and the average activities of our life together. *I love the feeling of having my hand held by Jake's as we drift off to sleep, noticing they meld together - you cannot feel any separation, their warmth is one sensation – it's like clouds passing and forming one shape together.*

Reading Surprised by Joy *by C.S. Lewis has been as pleasing as I expected. Thrilling me the most is hearing him discuss his being open to the "Homely" – that sense of wonder for the perfect quaint sites, the simple joys all around – so good to know someone else is touched like that. I want to help open Jake more in that regard of awareness, and see beauty in the smallest of things.*

It's a comfort to open this notebook up and see my familiar writing (sloppy as it is) and know who that is!

Giving myself permission to speak freely in my diaries gave me several benefits. I could get to the heart of issues and problems. I could listen to my feelings and honor them. In learning to listen, I developed that inner ear for hearing guidance from Spirit. That quiet soul deep within me would give me a nod, acknowledging that more of me was waking up. It was the gift from my Self of being saved from my shadow side. *My spirit reminds me how powerful it is when I let myself love myself, all of me, even if I have a lazy eye, a critical mind, a shy personality – to love all those things in total gives me such strength and clarity. Another thing to remember is that I often hide my Light – God how wonderful it is to see in others, as I'm uplifted by them – so is it service to let my brightness shine as well.*

How incredible God created things as beautiful and simple as gulls, tides, wind, seaweed. To sit with that scenery is very calming. Funny how the big waves hide below the surface and then plow ahead willfully. They remind me of me. The sunrise today practically made me cry. There was such brilliance in the curtains of light – bright pinks – streaks of color everywhere in very artistic forms...When I'm out walking I get so high and feel as if I own what I see. The beauty of the early fog in the valley is immense. The birds are glorifying God quite loudly outside – I join with them.

From the book Medicine Woman, "there is a seam dividing a human's two sides, each side serving a distinct purpose." I pondered what my weaker right side is all about. What does it mean to have a weak right eye? Why do problems materialize mostly on this side of my body???

I had my first official fairy dream! They asked me to go shopping for them!

It's odd how part of me has it together and feels so vibrant (like I got asked out at the store by a complete stranger), and the other part of me frantically picks at my fingers and has a tense back at times.

I love the words "tiff" and "spat," but Jake and I had one the other morning – we went to work without hugs or kisses – I felt awful.

The kitty went poop-scadiddily-doo-doo on my first 20 newly addressed wedding invitations!

I had another fairy dream. Something stopped me during the day and blew the memory into my mind because I didn't recall it first thing in the morning. I had seen almost a cloud or a shower of them in the air, circling and dancing. I waved in great joy at them.

With Jake so much in my mind, I am actually delirious to think of being with him for eons. I feel as if I hardly know him. It feels like we're doing something so new; the adventure and fear are there but also the great mystery of love and the awe of that. It's an odd feeling, making love and thinking you'll be with this person for a long time!

> Stone after stone
> the solid home is now built
> Today we walk inside
> where there is lots of light
> The rock has polished our hands
> Gentle fingers touch...
>
> The foundation moved once
> only to make for bigger doors
> Opening to green vistas
> Garden ground warming
>
> Let's take big pillows and
> witness the springtime
> from our porch
> The budding of our beautiful love

There was no runaway bride or groom with cold feet, and Jake and I actually got through the wedding ceremony smashingly. We had written our own vows and my brother composed a glorious wedding march. I remember waiting for my cue to enter the church, feeling overwhelmed and gushing with emotion, amazed that the moment had finally come. We had gone through so much. Our relationship up to this point had been like learning to drive with a clutch and balancing it with the gas pedal---we eventually sensed the right time to ease into it, and when to slowly release---to move forward together in a new direction. Except for the long wait for the catering company to bring out the food, the wedding went very well. *I felt like royalty in my wedding dress. Jake was prince material. A good number of people said it was the nicest wedding they've ever been to. Bob S. mentioned he never heard me promise to "obey" – ha! During the reception line my cheek throbbed from grinning.*

GREAT SAYING:
May the Great Mystery
make sunrise
in your heart.

Sioux Indian

ULTIMATELY ESPOUSED

Being married was one thing but being highly evolved was another. My usual personal struggles remained the same. I had made it over the hurdle of snagging the man I wanted, but I still needed to get the clutter out of my proverbial attic. I had the hormones that cried out for motherhood but also had the ones that made me bitchy and overly sensitive. I wrote, *Today is a sad day – I see how I am choosing this feeling – I do want to be lighter so it seems as if forgiveness is the sun in this situation. I feel I am in darkness. I feel fatter than I've ever felt and my skin is forever oily. It's not easy working on the inner stuff when you see so much that has to be corrected all over.*

I have been pondering my bent towards being critical – it seems critical (ha) that I change my attitude to be happy. I need to forgive myself for feeling afraid and wanting to hide. I see how that is the most important thing. It's also amazing how many past thoughts I listen to.

"Deep peace comes from meeting yourself and
your brothers totally without judgment."
"Your mind is the means by which you
determine your condition."
A Course in Miracles

I continued to be a seeker and, lucky for me, the community of Santa Barbara had a wonderful speaker named Jacob Glass who gave weekly talks on A Course in Miracles. Husband Jake joined me in being a "Course" student. Former boyfriend Eric was occasionally in attendance at the talks and updated me on how hard life was for him. He wasn't having successful relationships and he was wearing himself out with political action. I mentioned, *I see that forgiveness seems ever and ever more important, yet it is difficult when he is touched with the sadness at seeing the madness. (Eric has such a power over me, even after 4 years!)* Jacob's messages gave me some hearty spiritual vitamins that infused me with a dose of correct thinking. My journal depicted many uplifting moments as in: *There's the heavenly feeling that I can do or not do anything and I am still loved... Spirit's duality feels good when, as I say "Thank you God," I get a chill that also feels very very warm.*

It's wonderful how I've been seeing the incredible beauty around me with much greater sparkle – I've read that's what happens when you learn to see.

Blessings come upon me every day and I don't know if it's because I'm opening to God's love more, or if I am working for it by doing certain good works. In any case, I am coming to know the angel in me.

I was opening more broadly to God but was often confused about what to believe. Why were awful things happening and why were humans cruel? Why were some lives spared and others targeted for vicious brutality? Being raised a Unitarian-Universalist helped me keep my mind open, but what closed it were things like Catholic priests being child abusers, or terrible disasters striking some part of the world. I mourned, *I don't get it. My life is blessed, but 160,000 others' lives have just been snuffed. Out of that many people, certainly many were leading fulfilled journeys along the path. There were moms who loved their homes and families like I do. Their lives were just as important as mine. My life now seems so meaningless.*

Speaking of seeking: Jake and I joined a gathering of many seekers from all over the world when the gospel choir that I sang with was invited to Findhorn, a famous spiritual and ecological community in Scotland. Our group performed at an international conference over one Easter break, and Jake and I were able to attend some workshops that focused on life purpose and greeting the divine. There was no doubt that an expansive, powerful love energy hovered in the halls and gardens at Findhorn. It didn't seem to be within just our small bubble of experience; it appeared that nearly everyone was in love with everyone else. The air nearly hummed with the electric charge of loving tolerance and nonjudgmental attitudes. My devoted husband was overcome with feelings for another woman and held hands with her, and I flirted with the idea of having a massage from a cute New Zealand man---even though Jake and I were just newlyweds of two years. It was a bit like how I imagine heaven might be, where love flowed freely between races and genders, ignored age and marital status, and elevated one's mind and spirit.

Findhorn is renowned for many things besides being a spiritual center, and in particular it is a Mecca for gardeners. Plants and flowers grew bountifully in the sand, and residents at the community claimed that beings known as devas helped everything thrive despite harsh conditions. I was delighted to be there to enhance my fairy connection, and had the chance to visit a popular forest frequented by others who also hoped to see fairies. After much effort and concentration I finally gave up my quest, but in doing so I saw an unusual flash of light. I questioned whether or not I had conjured the vision but felt deep down that I had made actual contact with the fairy kingdom. *Once I surrendered I appreciated the depth of my sensitivity for feeling the presence of God in nature, and I developed a newfound self-love.*

♦ ♦ ♦ ♦ ♦ ♦ ♦

With insight came growth. With responsibility came challenge. With change came resistance! I was getting many opportunities for both resisting and learning lessons at work. Having risen from secretary to office manager at Work Training Programs, a non-profit agency providing services to the disabled, I faced many trials that helped me improve my skills in conflict resolution while supervising the office staff. Here were my various team members: a former alcoholic at age thirteen; a drug addict and thief who took off with the company's petty cash; a girl who chatted incessantly (mostly about her disappointing boyfriend); a gal who called in sick often; a young woman who was hyper and judgmental about her co-workers; a girl who had an undisclosed handicap (her brain didn't seem to turn on); and finally, a young lady with cerebral palsy whose speech was hard to understand and who, when upset, would spit and snort. Believe it or not, I even had one employee, Richard, who had been a manager for THE MONKEES! I met this guy a little too late! He had fabulous tales about his tours with the group and even recounted smoking with Jimi Hendrix the night before Jimi died. Richard also mentioned that he briefly dated Maureen McCormick who played Marcia on "The Brady Bunch."

My employees were effective teachers for prompting me to withhold judgment, be patient and firm, keep a sense of humor and balance out the stress. One of my harder tasks was to have compassion for myself when I made mistakes, and this mission has remained difficult for me. *I am hard on myself about doing something wrong, about not being perfect all the time. I allow guilt to remain with me longer than necessary when presented with an error.*

Working among the disabled gave me greater compassion for humanity as I watched the students strive for independence. Work Training Programs' population had a broad range of disabilities within it such as cerebral palsy, mild to moderate mental retardation, schizophrenia, autism, Down's syndrome, spina bifida and bipolar disorder. As a front office staff person I was able to "see it all," and my interactions with so many types of clients often made for interesting employment. One client was obsessed with earthquakes and stopped by daily to fiddle with his hands and comment that there would be a big one coming soon. Another young man told you what day of the week you were born if you told him your birth date. One girl who was helping the office staff by typing suddenly shrieked, and having scared everyone half to death, remarked that she had just broken a nail. (However, she was so bright that she appeared on the TV show "Name That Tune.")

These clients had some of the saddest case histories. One little sweetie was found as an abandoned baby in a trashcan. Many of the mental health clients had very disturbing family relations that involved neglect and molestation. It wasn't difficult for me to get attached to this bunch, and watching those who graduated to a higher level every year was extremely touching. It was common for the severely disabled to die young but it was a shock when a death did occur. When one woman of twenty-five died, I kept repeating her name over and over as if I could make better sense of what had happened. The students made such an impression on me, stealing my heart, that I still remember most of their names and can picture their unique faces, even eight years after leaving the job. (Speaking of earthquakes, that kid had been right! On 1/17/94 the Northridge earthquake struck at 4.35 am with a magnitude of 6.6. There were literally hundreds of aftershocks. I hated going to bed for a few weeks.)

I was riding over not only the waves of earthquakes but also the regular hills and valleys of life. One alarming low was a family member's attempted suicide on Mother's Day, followed later by the savage rape of a friend's friend. As I faced the dark side of human nature, I seriously contemplated whether it made sense to have a child. The world presented so many threats and I worried about the future. Once I made up my mind, I wanted a child badly, whether the planet would sustain us or not. Getting pregnant was troublesome because I hadn't ovulated for three months. *Hoping to conceive soon, every month feels like such a roller coaster. I'm trying to believe that I'm not scared about the whole adventure, and to accept that I deserve a child and am worthy of one. It was practically stressful this month, making sure to give ourselves enough opportunities for making a baby!*

For most of my days I anxiously await signs of pregnancy. I'm afraid to put all my energy into faith and prayer, in case I'm let down, and if I completely let go I'm afraid I'm not trying and doing my part to help create it. I do know I must trust the way God works it out.

Getting my period I grieved and felt anger and considered myself dumb and incompetent. After five months of trying you'd think we'd get it right.

It's been almost a year and I still haven't cleared myself of my feelings about the abortion. I hide the truth and hide from it as well. I keep my true emotions from Jake, afraid I'll feel like such a little girl. I rationalize and deny so much of what I feel. I am overly guided by what I fear others will think – it's incredible how much credence I give "others." Ultimately I must realize my own goal is God, regardless of whether or not it includes being pregnant.

I took some natural remedies but they didn't do the trick. Then I tried Chinese herbs that smelled and tasted awful, but in three weeks the doctor had me ovulating. (Drinking that stinky horrible concoction three times a day was nearly enough to make me change my mind.) In the meantime, I was participating in a new spiritual curriculum. It featured components of psychotherapy that were helping to bring me further insights about myself. I obviously hadn't finished taking out the trash. *I was shown in meditation how I'll try my damnedest to do everything because I feel the need to avoid ANY criticism - I'll strive endlessly to be a super woman. Plus, I miss the times of being so clear that I could come up with answers inside.*

I'm awfully afraid of accidentally harming my future baby – dropping it etc. – and the visions are horrifying. I'm afraid I don't eat right. I feel guilty I don't exercise. I haven't saved any money. Already I'm a nervous person – how will I be as a mom? It's not okay to be nervous – my teacher had asked if I felt nervous– why does it bug me SO MUCH to be told I'm nervous??? I'm disturbed by being human.

It's amazing how easy it is for me to choose hell over peace. Last night I fell into a depression upon eating 6 cookies and having a cup of homemade Kahlua™ liqueur. All day today I was miserable, feeling so guilty, fat and lazy. How funny it is now! I seek the inner comfort in knowing that whatever I do is okay. It's okay to eat 6 cookies, and to eat 10 more tomorrow. Father, I release to your Holy Spirit my unwillingness to see myself in a holy loving way.

As seen in my frequent ups and downs with Jake, I jumped around often in the bounce house of life. I went up and down emotionally so many times in my pursuit of pregnancy that it was a wonder I wasn't nauseated all the time. Month after month I was exhausted by hoping too much and trying too hard. I remarked, *Once again I am fooled by the normal signs and am not carrying a child, although I do continue to be laden in my thoughts of having to have one. I simply dread the coming of another period.*

My dear husband was a trooper in helping me with the baby-making "project" and I was increasingly in love with him. I wrote about how positively gorgeous Jake would look, and while making love once, I had a glimmer of time travel back to Egyptian times where Jake had surely been a prince. In that dream I had the mystical awareness that we shared a most amazing love that was greater than most – a bond for eternity.

THE CHEMISTRY OF SEX

Lo and behold, there was the blue dot! What little soul has picked me? After seven months of trying to conceive, there I was, looking at my home pregnancy test stick several times to make sure the indicator was confirming my greatest desire. Then I proceeded to shriek, hop and shout hallelujah. Apparently I had conceived on Valentine's Day (awwwwwww). In celebration, and also to see if I needed to focus on any particular issues, I selected an Angel Card and was amazed to see the Angel of Expectancy. How incredible was that?!

Just when I thought I could discontinue the yucky Chinese herbs, my doctor advised me to keep taking them to prevent miscarriage and morning sickness. The herbs honestly didn't help with the latter. I felt awful in the mornings and moved about two-tenths of a mile per hour. I mentioned, *Some days are so bad, I just sit. That's it. This has been a month of many naps. I'm adjusting to not being productive and busy.* Maternity undies were a riot and went way up to the bottom of my breasts. In the passing months I got to know all about what comes bundled with pregnancy: leg muscle spasms during the night, hip pain, numb hands during sleep, major fatigue and no heaping desire for sex. (Putting a heating pad under my bottom helped me get in the mood only a little, and fantasizing about handsome actors helped just a little more.) In spite of these physical discomforts I absolutely loved being pregnant, compared with some women who couldn't wait for pregnancy to be over. I loved resting my arms on top of my round tummy and I delighted feeling so "in the moment" when a good kick went wham against my insides.

Jake and I had a bit of trouble adjusting to our new world that was around the corner. He was busy with the foundation of the new house in the back, and I was busy cooking up the kid and reading pregnancy books. I wanted to be pampered and yet left alone. *I have felt "shy" when he touches me, and many times I don't like to be kissed. I thought Tauruses were earthy and sensual. What we could use is more romance – it's been so "routine" with talk about the house, organizing the baby room, etc. – we are getting along more like roommates. Sex is still a problem, one that bothers me the most. I have NO hormones in my body that will give me the desire. And it's weird how I get so moody when I'm tired.*

I reminded Jake about the upcoming class at the hospital for expectant parents. "I think it's silly to take the Baby Basics class," he commented. "Everything should just come naturally – you'll know what to do."

"No way! There are so many things that could go wrong. I've been studying a lot, but we should still go. Definitely!" Riled much?

During the baby class Jake nearly fainted during the C-section video. I considered having a home delivery but decided that for our first baby, I wanted to be in the safety of a hospital. Home births were very popular and cool those days but I was too nervous to go for it. *It is remarkable to realize a real human being is living inside me. I wonder how we've chosen to go through labor and delivery together. As baby gets bigger I wear down more quickly. But I'm so happily pregnant, proud of my usual good health and lovely rotundness, awaiting the appearance of the being within. I suppose there is a bit of reluctance to give up this big beautiful belly – it's safer with the baby on the inside, less to handle – so nice to rub and pat, with only **clean** diapers around...*

During the long wait, there were the regular postings in my journal of lives running their normal course. I wrote, *A myriad of thoughts and feelings are upon me. Funny how I always know when I need journal therapy.*

It does amaze me how hard it is for Jake to pay attention to details. I realized today that I do observe so much – it does make me the writer.

In visiting with Dad, God's loving presence was SO strong that I was cheering inside for how nourished I felt. His love was good for me and the baby! How blessed it was, to see a change, and in whom it took place I know not.

Dear Holy Spirit, I am moved when I can hear Your advice for the simple things – the precautions here and there – but I ask you to take me further in being a student more open to Your Truth.

Doing lots of gardening. It's such a tremendous joy to me to experience God in this way – laboring but loving it, and being centered in the luxury of free time and choice. I wish for Jake to be able to know this kind of happiness – I get so filled...

Have been working with <u>A Course in Miracles</u> on my holiness and that around me – it's amazing what a gentleness there is to everything when I give that kind of attention to the world and myself (which are the same thing!).

I dreamt I was looking at the garden and I saw fairies – they were clearer than I'd ever seen or dreamt before – first they were a swirling cloud of violet light around a plant, and then I saw tiny figures in the cloud, dancing and blessing the plant.

"... everything that slows us down and forces patience, everything that sets us back into the slow cycles of nature, is a help. Gardening is an instrument of grace."

May Sarton

The slow process of the incredible baby-making miracle inside me reminded me of those soaps I loved as a kid. They were the kind that you impatiently used over and over to get to the special thing buried inside, be it a cute toy or cheap party favor object. Month after long, tiring month, I was eager to get to my very own special thing buried inside. When birth drew closer, waiting to deliver the baby was like waiting for the change in the sky between dawn and sunrise, or for the moon to go into an eclipse. I knew any second the change would occur and the thrilling anticipation put me on edge. Any moment my brain would realize that the climax was NOW and great energy would be released. I recalled after the birth, *My water broke at 2:30 am and I started to shake from chills of fear and the unknown. What would this be like??? Regular contractions began immediately, lasting 30-45 seconds every three minutes almost on the dot. Ginseng and raspberry tea seemed to speed the labor.* Getting my girth into the car to go to the hospital and trying to sit comfortably was very hard, and I remember wanting to leap out of the car so that I could stretch my belly out. As soon as we arrived at Cottage Hospital, I got out and threw up in the bushes.

I was lucky. Labor lasted only six hours and I delivered a healthy baby drug-free. The cute OB-GYN threw up her hands in a big "ta da!" I had heard some **wicked** horror stories about the troubles of birthing. One surprising story concerned the delivery of a baby to a very large woman in my town who had no idea that she was pregnant.

THE BABYHOOD OF DANYA

Little Danya (rhymes with Tanya) came onto the scene crying loudly. I felt exquisite joy and relief when my newborn's slippery body was placed onto my chest. It didn't matter that my underside had ripped and needed stitching; it didn't matter that my mom and husband had seen me all exposed and gooey; all that mattered was that Danya had arrived safe and sound with all the right body parts. Unfortunately she did have jaundice, and Jake and I gave her home phototherapy treatments for a few days. Our baby had to spend most of the time lying in a sort of tanning booth wearing only booties and an eye mask. It was a heartache to see our infant alone in that contraption, but at least we could be grateful that Danya wasn't born under the same conditions as I was: arriving more than a month premature, weighing only three pounds, and being stuck in the hospital for six weeks.

More troubling than the jaundice was the fact that Danya didn't breastfeed until she was two weeks old. Being an exhausted new mom, I discovered that having a cranky non-nursing baby created plenty of stress. In order to properly feed and train the baby, I had to first pump my milk (ouch) and then wear a bottle around my neck from which two tubes hung that were taped onto both nipples. The baby then nursed out of a tube while simultaneously getting accustomed to the breast. This ordeal of rigging the bottle to my body occurred numerous times during the day. Once Danya did nurse on her own, her sharp nails ripped at my nipples (EEEK). When the baby spit up, milk got into the folds of her neck and smelled disgusting, like very old whipped cream. Not only did I have fatigue, nipple soreness and concern about Danya's weight, I also suffered ear pain from the baby's piercing, loud howls. Danya seemed to cry more than she slept. I took the baby on rides in the car to get her to sleep. Other solutions that helped settle the colicky baby were putting her in her baby seat on top of the dryer, or covering her with a blanket that had been warmed in the dryer.

I told Danya's proud grandmother, "I went to our Lamaze class reunion, and no one else mentioned having a fussy baby. I was so bummed! Mine was the only one who was crying and all the others were sleeping." I jotted down a few other early comments from my bumpy initiation into motherhood: *I love how, when I get her body lined up to nurse, she swats my chest, pawing like a cat. It's an amazing job for a woman to do – feed all day (every two hours), get poor sleep, keep the house up – wow!*

Danya didn't like baths, so she screamed and got very red in the face! She looked right at me, as if I were a torturer.

One of the things I loved best about having a baby was carrying her around like a very special package (nearly an appendage), and caressing her beautifully formed, smooth bald head. She also had a most deliciously sweet smell to her skin, and frankly, I was proud as hell to have made her.

From what I had read about newborns, I established that we had a "high-need baby" on our hands. Some studies show that these types of kids become quite intellectual, so the notion of potentially high intelligence did give me comfort when the going got rough and the demands felt unbearable. I felt fairly certain that I never wanted to go through this ordeal again, but as Danya's personality began to emerge, being a mom became more fulfilling. *It is so deeply heart-warming how she'll look at us from the one parent's arms to the other parent so adoringly. She does the cutest thing where she raises a shoulder to her ear and grins, as if to say, "Look how darling I am."*

I've noticed more crying from wanting things – she'll look at me like, "Why are you not picking me up?"

I took delight in watching the baby's antics and trying to unscramble her communications. Part of the amusement was that, at one year, Danya was not walking but preferred scooting on her butt instead (just like her Uncle Scott, or "Scooter"). I discovered, as all mothers do, that checking on the preoccupations of small children and running after them made for good calisthenics. I found, *One of Danya's hobbies is knocking the magnets off the fridge. She also loves to bang open and shut the broiler door on the oven. If I want to keep her busy a little while, I just give her a tube of toothpaste – she loves to open the cap and put her finger in for a taste!*

The other day I laughed hard because Danya was happily playing in the bathtub and she suddenly said what sounded like "Fajita!" – although quite often her language sounds more Chinese.

I love it when she holds out her hand for something and flexes her fingers in a beckoning gesture.

She loves to reorganize the spice rack. If she sees the swing on the floor she'll drag it to us. Danya kicks in great excitement to be held by her dad.

Part of my wonderment at parenting was observing the rapid development of Danya's language. As historian of our baby's growth I kept busy keeping current in the kid's journal and there was plenty to document: *She says "mee mow" for Mickey Mouse. Another phrase she has adopted is "herego" when she hands us something for "here ya go." She loves to walk to the edge of the driveway and sit and collect pebbles – she'd do it for a good half-hour if you let her. She loves to ask for raisins – "more raeree." Danya says "uppie" a lot to sit on the bathroom counter if we're in there.*

It's great when she crawls into my lap when she's ready for books.

She says her name often at the start of a sentence like, "Danya ball go slide." Whenever she wants something she says so, but without the word want: "I-more" or "I-macookie."

Once our daughter reached the age of two I made sure to write down Danya's hilarious comments: *Danya surprises us more and more by her language, memory and talent. She says perfect sentences like, "Don't drive too fast Mommy."*

I asked my little girl once, "Are you ready for a bath?"
She replied, "I don't think so."

I love her translations of words – sometimes I have to make many guesses to figure her out. "Pah cus" is popsicles. "Doeluh" is stroller (those s's are so hard). The "sm" combo is also difficult – she says "mokes" for smoke.

Her best friend is "fwaapie" for Floppy Bunny. She's snuggled up on her side with Bunny resting between her shoulder and her chin. *Dear God I'll never thank you enough.*

Her language has become more complex now, as in, *"I help Mommy make dinner pretty soon."* This morning she was noticing how Bunny and Mommy have a little nose and she said, *"Daddy has a big nose."*

Of course, toddlerhood wasn't all patty-cake and bunnies. As much as Danya was an absolute joy, she was also a terror. I had a plethora of miserable moments created by the moody monster that inhabited our daughter's body: *She was the worst tonight I've ever seen. After dinner she wouldn't take a bath, get dressed or brush teeth without a **major** battle at each step. It's amazing how intense she can be, curling up on the ground when upset and trying to win her way. It takes great strategy, creativity and sheer trickery to get her to do things at times...*

She's finally settled into her bigger bed after a week of hell. It would take us from 8:30-10:15 to get her off to sleep. She'd get up about 8 times until it finally registered in her brain that it was bedtime.

She had a huge tantrum on our vacation (we had to close the windows, it was so severe). I got so alarmed at her intensity that I was sobbing. Danya was hysterical and Jake was holding her to get her to calm down. She's had terrible fits before, but this one really made me feel anxious about her mental / emotional health.

Danya was just a normal child who had occasional meltdowns. Later on I would wonder if perhaps she was subconsciously reacting to the trouble that her parents were having. I was suddenly having an affair.

TO HELL AND BACK

Charles turned up at my work as a computer consultant. He was a bit funny looking but charming as hell. He made me laugh by quoting lines from Woody Allen movies and he had a sharp intellectual side as well. He loved the same band I had adored for years. He paid me some serious attention, and at the time, my poor husband was working too hard to be able to do the same thing. It all started when I went out to lunch with Charles (first to discuss business and then to flirt) and we shared wonderful vegetarian meals together. He flattered me at work and left witty and provocative notes on my desk. Originally I assumed that Charles would become just a friend of mine as well as Jake's. Whoops. I was unable to stop thinking about Charles. Once I succumbed to his request for a kiss, he was no longer simply a friend. If only I had turned him down.

What was so pathetic about the situation was that Jake was constructing the new house for our family at the time. He was working for our future and I was tearing it down. I had been feeling burned out as a mother and unappreciated in general, and the enchanting "boyfriend" gave me a big ego boost. I enjoyed the workings of Charles's keen mind to a great extent, but I was particularly entranced by the way he wrote so romantically. It didn't matter that he had thin lips and a nasally voice; I couldn't resist the physical attraction he held for me. He had nice biceps from playing squash. Charles ended up paling as a lover in comparison to Jake, but the anticipation of sex with an intriguing guy was too alluring for me. Whenever I was feeling overworked at home, I got an energy lift to think about how Charles was courting me. I should have been thinking, "I'm married, I'm married," but instead my thoughts were, "He really likes me, and it makes me feel great." In a way, having this secret alter ego helped me feel more animated with Danya. I was a doting mother who already gave much of my time to enhance Danya's learning, and frequently brought home library books on crafts and games to do together; yet having a lover on the side temporarily infused me with vixen vitality and thus more energy to share with my child. I became a younger woman within my thirty-two-year-old body. I was, temporarily, a big time sleaze girl.

Later I grasped that Danya had really taken over as the love of my life since her birth, and that my poor husband had become number two. Perhaps I had carried some deep-seated resentments towards Jake for all of his past indecisiveness, and a part of me was getting back at him through the affair, which was so ugly to even think about. My equilibrium was completely off balance, and those exuberant feelings that paired with romantic love for Charles fogged my vision. During the period when I lived at home with Jake but had liaisons with Charles, I battled with torn emotions and wrote, *I have seen such great upheaval that never before have I taken so many Tums™. I get headaches and bad stomach cramps. My guilt and remorse twist my insides. The pain comes and goes and at times I feel I can't get enough air and that I get close to heaving. How much of a fool am I to have fallen in love with Charles - what percent?* I had been so skillful in acting like a caring companion to Jake, and crafted clever lies to mask my deceitful behavior. All for my ego, the Tempting Trickster.

When Jake discovered my sinful actions, he was a saint for not kicking me out, and he was a trooper to agree to join me in counseling. His Libra trait of loyalty was something I would treasure forever. He even brought his adulterous wife hot tea when I was sick in bed. Despite the discomfort in our relationship, he learned to be more present with his emotions. When Jake found an unfinished letter I had started to Charles, he reacted strongly, and even though it was a miserable situation, I felt grateful that he was in touch with his feelings. "Damn you, damn you, damn you! I can't believe you would do this! How can you act this way? I hate this!" he yelled. *I went to bed feeling like I couldn't take the hell anymore, and at 2am I sat up and realized the decision had come to me with little effort. Danya saved us. My considering her future helped me decide not to make things stressful on her. I had a wonderful husband. Charles wasn't worth it.*

In counseling, I learned again that I keep my feelings and thoughts inside, particularly the ones I'm scared to be open about. Jake heard the tape that was made from my private session and he discovered some painful things that shocked him. He understands me better and still respects me! I love him for his willingness and his capacity to adapt every day to the stuff that comes up. He deserves a ton of credit for being so caring and for trying to understand.

In therapy I shook with fear and anger, mostly at Mom and Dad and at myself. I'm so annoyed that I carry so much of my past – it's very debilitating.

Whew. There were parts to Charles that I hadn't yet seen. If I had chosen the path of taking off with my lover, I would have started a life with a con man with borderline personality disorder. He believed that he was above all of the rules. Charles ended up being convicted of embezzlement and went to prison.

DUO NUEVO

The short affair that brought such turmoil into our lives actually strengthened our marriage. Jake and I were now a better team. We knew what we needed to improve in ourselves and in our lives together. We knew what a gift it was to have Danya, and we found new pleasure in being united as parents. It would have been a shame if either of us had missed any part of Danya's precious childhood. I documented some episodes with our three-year-old: *She scraped her knee and was very upset, yet she seemed to enjoy watching herself cry in the mirror.*

It's fun to go through her books and change words once in awhile to see how she reacts – she always corrects me! Danya is also very good at learning songs. She knew that I'd skipped "the dog takes the cat" in the Farmer in the Dell.

I offered, "Doodles, I'll make you a deal. If you eat three more spoons of sweet potatoes, you can have more cheese popcorn."

"I don't want to make that deal."

Funny, if I need for her to be ready to leave the house she may say, "Not yet. Pretty soon."

Lately she's been asserting her desires ever more strongly. We'll explain why it's not okay to _____ and she'll say, "But I WANT to!"

Jake was trying to brush her teeth one night. He said, "Sweetie, move your tongue out of the way."

"That's where it goes, Dad. It's supposed to stay in my mouth."

Illness suddenly zapped the fun, and having a sick child made me feel utterly miserable. Danya came down with scarlet fever. Her high temperature spiked for a week, but the real curse of the illness was the accompanying herpes simplex. The sores on her gums were so painful she could hardly eat for a few days. We were both crying in

111

the pharmacy while waiting for a prescription. Once Danya recovered though, we were back to dressing up in glamorous outfits and making cakes out of sand and dirt and berries. The funny little kid stories continued. *I asked if she could help me put pine needles around some plants and she told me, "I think I can handle that." We talked about putting the plants in their bed and she wanted to know, "Where's the sun's bed?"*

We were talking about God and she remarked, "You gotta dream about Him until you know His name." (Hmmm! What exactly was she learning at day care?)

*Danya gets real particular when dressing her dolls – she'll instruct, "No, you gotta put that on like **this**!"*

At times I could see why some people don't wish to be parents. Kids require so much time and effort and money and energy. A parent has to struggle with giving up their interests to some degree, making many adjustments over many years. But when those "firsts" come--- the first time your child writes to Santa, ties their shoes, balances on a bike, gives their first book report, goes to the first dance---those moments reign supreme! They melt your heart, swell your pride, make you jump for the camera...and they help blot out your memory of those awful seconds in the grocery store when your kid was a brat and caused a scene. Touching moments will hit you even when you're simply watching TV and you want to cry, because the commercial with the mother and baby really captures the beauty of parental love; or because the "Winnie the Pooh" episode was especially heartfelt; or because tragedy separated a child from its guardian. Children have such a simple sweetness to share with us.

Danya's asking WHY questions sure keeps my mind busy.

One time when she was sick with a cold, she woke up in the night crying every hour. At one point she was sobbing, "Mommy there's no picture on the wall of a dog!" Whoa.

She pronounces the 1st meal of the day as "breppest." She also says, "This be's over here" or "She be's a ballerina."

While playing hide and seek I'd found a simple place that fooled her, so while she kept looking she spoke out, "Mommy, you're good at this!"

*Danya was "cytek" [excited] about Christmas and Santa's
coming. During the Christmas parade there were marchers in red and
white and she commented that they looked like Waldo!*

At this point in my story it was the early 1990's. Trouble was
encompassing the planet as usual. I noted, *The Soviet Union has
changed. Gorbachev has resigned. People who live in St. Petersberg
wait in lines as long as two to three miles trying to buy food. 700,000
people have been irradiated from Chernobyl. The war in El Salvador
has ended after* **twelve years**. *Dan Quayle had his Council on
Competitiveness designed to deregulate already weak environmental
policies. I have thus been having action/sci-fi war dreams this week.
One was where the feds were throwing heat-sensor bombs (balls that
acted like magnets to warm flesh) that were blowing people up.*

*It seems like the older I get, I see more cruelty and fear and
ignorance - things that deeply disturb me. There have been riots in LA
since the beating of Rodney King and the cops were acquitted. 2000
fires have been set and 36 people died. I break inside that these
nightmares exist in this civil society.*

*There has been a horrible civil war in Yugoslavia with more
than two million refugees. Florida had a hurricane and thousands are
homeless. Nicaragua had a 7.1 earthquake with a thirty-foot tidal
wave!*

◆ ◆ ◆ ◆ ◆ ◆ ◆ ◆

Since Danya had been a high-need baby, I was convinced one
child was plenty. For three tiring years I was completely certain that I
could only handle one child. I spoke with several people who were
"only children" and got mixed reviews. It wasn't until I visited a good
friend with four sweet kids that I changed my mind, determined that I
did indeed have enough love and energy to give to another baby.

Jake cautioned me, "You don't have to work so bloody hard at
it. If you didn't put such extreme dedication into parenting you would

have some energy left over. It'll be okay. Let's do it. It will be great and we shouldn't wait any longer."

While Jake and I worked on procreating, Danya gave us plenty of cute remarks and behaviors to jot down. *Her memory is so good that I can't put things past her. She'll remind me, "You promised!"*

I mentioned, "Doodles, you didn't eat much dinner. I want you to have a little more so you won't be hungry later."

"So what?"

She wants new things more often. My logic that she doesn't play with all that she has doesn't impress her or change her desire. Thank goodness for yard sales!

She told Dad during a bath that "Ariel her doll was 6 and 3 pennies." "Pennies," he said, "that's money," and she said, "But the other girl is 6 and 3 quarters!" I must point out that Danya had the cutest scratchy voice as a young child. I adored listening to her when she conversed with her dolls, or when she recited lines from the <u>Peter Pan</u> book on tape she had nearly memorized. When she was sounding especially animated, that froggy voice got squeaky.

Danya loves to gargle songs while brushing her teeth. She could really sit for a long time entertaining herself like that.

When I was leaving her room after saying good night, she said, "I'll love you forever... and that will never change."

Danya was talking to herself while playing with building blocks, and she casually commented, "Oh Jesus." Jake and I cracked up! Today when I picked her up at day care we forgot her lunch box and I told her God reminded me to go get it. She asked where God was and I said everywhere.

Jake, Danya and I went to the bank and Danya noticed that the yoga studio he goes to was next door. We asked her how she realized that it was there (the sign is pretty little) – it was because she had seen people in "their bending suits." Love it!

Regardless of how well things were going overall for our family, I still had issues with my husband and myself. I could be such a bull (portraying my Taurus attributes), and could also be totally full of bull. *It seems that every time Jake and I get in a tiff it's because of my complaints about something. I struggle with: do I keep things to myself more, especially since the stuff is usually so petty, or do I assert my needs with open honest communication?* Jake and I probably butted heads more from exhaustion than from being at odds, but there were quite a few times when I remember lying in bed and seeing clearly that men were so bloody different from women. Ladies, you know when you've felt that wall instantly rise up between you and a guy? During those strained moments I was convinced that my hubby and I couldn't think and feel on the same level, that our discussions were a lost cause, and that we wouldn't change. In any case, the act of juggling our copious responsibilities as working parents felt pretty overwhelming at times. My having a spouse certainly cut down on the stress (God bless single mothers!), and yet I chided myself, *Why should the constant work of child, shopping, dishes, food, job, etc. bother me, especially when I've only got one kid? I often feel taken for granted for being on the "home job" so much. We both feel we don't thank each other often enough... I've resolved to cut down on my interests.*

I'm so grateful Jake and I had the sense to hold on to each other, but sex is still a problem. It's never often enough for him. I start resenting that he still doesn't understand or do what I need, but I feel guilty and think he'll never change and I just have to "turn up the love."

Work has been incredibly demanding because I had to fire a woman after six days (she was sleeping at her desk) and I've been doing three peoples' jobs for four months.

I have had three dreams in a row of different men (one was a honey massage with Kevin Costner).

The challenges of a regular day, combined with the assortment of psycho mindsets that I had, contributed to my old habit of picking at my cuticles. If I felt any kind of roughness I had to nibble at it, or pull it off to make it smoother. Sometimes my smoothing adjustments made it worse. I would try to repair the damage and cause further coarseness, then bite and pick more. Minor bleeding didn't bother me. During winters when my skin was drier, the heels of my feet were crackly and I picked at the rough skin there as well. On occasion I was able to make the connection between what I was thinking and how I was attacking my flesh, and tried pinpointing the pressures that were gnawing at me. The picking behavior was an anxiety release mechanism that I could conveniently hide underneath tables, but my mom often sensed what I was doing and chastised me for not leaving my hands alone.

GIVING IT ANOTHER GO

For most of a year I was focused on making baby number two. Since Danya was already five, I wanted to work on closing that big gap of years between child one and child two. Once I put my mind to a plan I was relentless in the pursuit of carrying it out. *My biggest problem right now is having anything on my mind BUT thinking about being pregnant. If only I thought about God as much. I had to stop charting my temperature because it made me too obsessed.*

I ended up getting herbs and acupuncture for conception because my blood and kidneys were weak. These ingredients would open "the gates to the womb." I had tears of joy in gratitude for having God lead me to this treatment and for being open in myself to knowing what I needed.

It wasn't long before I missed a period. I went in for a pap and urine test. Moments later the doctor walked in saying, "Congratulations!"

"Oh, I hope you are right! Really?" (I didn't feel pregnant.) The physician then discovered a fetus but no heartbeat. My own heartbeat skipped a few beats on this rapid emotional ride and it was a second bummer that I needed a D&C to prevent infection. Despite this setback, Jake and I were faithful to that egg and sperm enterprise of making long-lasting fusion.

Traveling to Detroit to sing at a gospel music national convention took my mind off my miscarriage. I was still a proud member of Mama Pat's Inner Light Community Gospel Choir, and our small group joined with thousands of black singers who attended workshops and performed in a mass choir at the end of the convention. Those of us with white faces were few as we stood among the throng. I remember sweating profusely from the heat of the city that summer, but what stands out most from that special experience was the overpowering joy; I felt nestled in the arms of a magnificent love that seemed to ooze from every singer. This jubilant crowd blew me away with their devotion and tenderness as they worshipped, celebrated, and boogied to some dynamite tunes.

Fall then came around with its tremendous glory, and was not only a beautiful distraction from the pregnancy effort but was also a pleasant source of inspiration. *It's quite breezy now and cool and I rejoice in the coming of fall. I simply revel in it, and wonder what my soul has experienced in the past to love it so. I feel such deep deep joy for this season. Thank God I can recognize and appreciate beauty – there's so much of it – the sweet face of my husband, the soft cheek of my child, the bright showy leaves overhead.* Fall meant pretty leaves and it also meant the holidays and party food. I was an absolute sucker for homemade Christmas cookies. I complained about having gained five pounds and tried being aware of my thoughts of lowered self-esteem, and worked on keeping a positive outlook by using different affirmations.

"I place my future in the hands of God."
<u>A Course in Miracles</u>

The statement above was my favorite mantra for helping me surrender my need for control. It gave instant succor. It served as a safety net to catch me when my ego threw me over the rocky cliffs of emotional unbalance. Using it was like taking the yellow brick road and knowing with certainty that the wizard would straighten everything out. I also had to affirm to myself, "I WANT THE PEACE OF GOD" and that I didn't have to be pregnant to have it.

The new year got off to a weird start. Danya's day care teacher thought she had breast cancer but didn't. One of my co-workers did indeed have cancer. My friend's uncle had the "flesh-eating disease" and was losing limbs, and a girl at work had flipped over in her car six times. I thought I had a virus. Instead, my home pregnancy test came out positive! I felt gushy with delight. My morning sickness wasn't quite as bad the second time, although on occasion my illness made me poke out my tongue in discomfort over the next few months. As much as I loved being pregnant and saw it as a grand cosmic experience, it wasn't all easy and breezy. I groused, *I feel like I'm supposed to be in my calm center all the time but that's impossible. One of the cats has been spraying in the house and I want to squish him so badly! I feel guilty and apologize to the baby for being this angry.*

At eight months I got up about eight times a night (sometimes twelve), just to pee out a few droplets. On my walks I had attacks of ligament pain.

So close to birthing now. I wouldn't mind being pregnant for three more months just to feel like it hasn't gone so fast. Part of me will be relieved when it's over, as the physical conditions have been uncomfortable and challenging – the rest of me wants to languish in the specialness of it.

I had to ask angels to help me with my anxiety – I had been feeling worried that the baby would come while I'm still sick (very congested), and so I felt like I was sending a lot of No messages to the baby. The Angel of Tenderness helped me relax. Mary the midwife said it's normal to do "housecleaning" at the end, and that I'll have all the strength I need when the time comes. I'm really forcing myself not to do too much.

THE ARRIVAL OF A VERY BOYISH GIRL

At midnight I woke Jake up and said, "This is it."

"Oh wow, it is? What happened?"

"I've had terrible cramps, been restless for an hour, then I threw up the protein bar I just ate."

He phoned the midwives while I soaked in the bathtub. Then I felt best walking around the room, kneeling at the bed, rocking my hips back and forth and groaning. Towels and dropcloths had been placed around the bedroom. *I tried biting on a washcloth so I wouldn't moan too much and scare Danya, but I had to groan and grunt anyway! It hurt quite a bit but the anticipation of the baby's being born made it tolerable.*

Birthing at home was dramatically different; the lighting was soft, I had every comfort nearby, Jake could lie next to me in bed, and my mom could wake up the first born down the hall when the time came. I tried squeezing two combs into my thumbs; it was a technique that was supposed to help the pain but didn't. The midwives were like goddesses, floating about giving encouragement and tenderly providing every facet of support. Jake was a fabulous coach as well. I squeezed the dickens out of his hand and swatted him if he tried touching my belly. He cheered me on with, "You are so strong, Lili. What a lovely, powerful woman you are. You are doing great. Keep going. You are so strong. The baby is almost here." I craved his comforting words, using them for an energy surge like a shot of espresso to help me focus. Some moments were such a struggle to keep going that I leaned on Jake's reassurance as a weary mountain climber would rest against a hillside, desperate to see the summit. Finally, the baby arrived after less than four hours of labor. *The baby came out "in the bag" which indicates a future as a wise teacher. I only had to push for twenty minutes! BOY it feels so great when the body slides out. I held the baby for five minutes and then I was dying to know the sex.*

Many people were certain I'd have a boy. We had thought it'd be Logan or Evan, but instead it was Tessa! [Her boyishness will be revealed later.]

It was so lovely being at home with candles and all the necessary comforts, without nurses and noise and interference. The midwives brought me a lovely tray with yogurt, fruit and nuts. Oh fiddle! Piffle! Now I had a second baby who wasn't any good at latching on either!

I didn't have to use those blasted feeding tubes with Tessa. We needed only a few days with a good lactation consultant and we were on our way to happy nursing sessions. Tessa was a chipper little newcomer, but Danya needed to ease into the arrangement of losing some attention. I read somewhere that siblings were closer to their brother or sister if they were present at the baby's birth. It wasn't surprising though that Danya made comments about sending Tessa back, or putting her in the trash. Yet as soon as Tessa was old enough, the girls were having baths together. It seemed that Danya liked to "play" with Tessa, but that word was a loose term referring to her decorating the baby with odd objects like underwear or pouring water on her head.

I gathered up more sweet young baby stuff to write about during the next year. *Tessa says "ging." What a great word! If she sees the cat she'll put out her hand and say, "Meng" sort of. She has a motion of sweeping or swiping that she uses sometimes to retrieve a desired object. Pretty comical.*

Tessa cries whenever Daddy's holding her and he sneezes. She likes the sound of fortune cookies in their wrappers. Nammy (Grandma) calls her "Windy Bottom" for her gaseousness.

At one year of age she says "ba" for ball, balloon, box, and book. She'll say "Ree buh" and get in my lap for a book. Cookie is "jurgie."

You can ask her nearly any question and she'll say "Yeah." Danya will joke and ask, "Daddy is so horrible, right?" and Tessa will answer, "Yeah."

Once her hair had grown in, Tessa had the prettiest, thick

blond curls. She looked like she had an expensive perm. Brushing it was another matter!

Tessa likes moving objects around, like taking things out of cabinets – her newest trick is putting odd things in the trash, like Danya's new schoolbook or our tenant's RENT CHECK all crumpled up!

She's addicted to "pig bears" – picking berries – her poop is so black cuz she eats gobs at a time.

Time passed so quickly. I wasn't keeping up with my own journal like I used to, and I felt ashamed that Tessa wasn't getting the same special treatment that Danya had received. Jake had started a new career and was gone a lot. I summed it up, *I feel guilty about the way I'm raising the "second child" who is indeed suffering from being the second - fewer notes, pictures and videos are being taken! Life seems like a whirlwind with the busyness of caring for two kids and pretending to maintain the house (it's SO gross)...*

This woman has been quite crazy. I'm able to function as a mom just fine but NOT as a contented wife, lover, friend. Once again the same problem of my "doing it all" has come back – I don't do well with this one. When will I learn? Jake's been working insane hours in the field and I don't like the burden it puts on me. To top it off, I'm working so hard that I feel he should pamper me or be extra sweet or thank me or something – he just acts like business as usual. I feel I should accept the situation better and be the devoted partner no matter what...

Jake got the message. *For one weekend I had a great view... of myself! Jake took the girls to his mom's and I got to be alone. It was very filling. I annointed myself with contentment. I was chock full of bliss about my joy of being in this particular family, and felt recharged as a mother. I took the time to listen longer to my center. It was especially fun deciding just for me when to go to bed, when to wake up and what to do with my many magical moments. Thank you Spirit for allowing me space to be more present with you. God, I thank you – thought I should let you know.*

Now I am married to a forty-year-old who braved a vasectomy (yea!!!). I have a two-year-old and an eight-year-old. I feel rather satisfied with my life – to die soon would be tragic but at least I have felt the glory of God and seen His beauty. My daughters are gorgeous and give me total joy, despite whining and a few nagging problems. I love my job, house, town, hubby. Am exercising more, making fresh juices, and look better with lighter hair.

The kids continued to entertain. My notebooks had some more good material, so bear with me, please, as I make you wade through more journal entries. I'm just a proud mommy who finds these passages amusing and I insist on leaving them in.

At the beach in Big Sur there was a sign that showed NO CAMPING (a triangle tent symbol) and Danya, proud to be paying attention to signs and reading them, said, "No witches' hats?!" Hilarious. Tessa was developing her speech and "whit" meant fish!

Danya loved to ask Tessa,"What does a cow say?" Tessa usually got it right, but occasionally she would respond, "A bottle."

I admire Danya's wanting to help shift Tessa's bad moods by pretending to hurt herself a little. It usually makes Tessa giggle to see her sister smacking into walls with a resolute "OWWW."

Danya has had such a fear of riding her bike despite our several previous practice attempts. This time she prepared herself by getting into sweats with wristbands, kneepads and a fanny pack with bandaids and Tylenol™!

We asked Tessa how old she is the other day and she said, "Two minutes."

"Keppitch" stands for ketchup. "Washing macleaner" is obvious. "Breksuff" stood for breakfast (compared to Danya's "breppest"). Tessa seemed to be making up words and came up with "forkmcdiddie."

She likes to cover up the cat with pillows and he hates it.

I like it when Tessa says (if she's tired), "I'm full of walking."

Tessa likes to make drawings (mostly colored stripes), roll up the paper, ask us to close our eyes and then she sings "Happy Birthday." Once when the girls dressed up as princesses Tessa admired herself in the mirror and remarked, "I definitely look beautiful."

Meanwhile, back at the ranch (or psycho farm), I was still not feeling in total harmony with the universe. *I've been a bit of a mess lately but I suppose it's always good to suffer as it leads me closer to Spirit. I feel disconnected to myself, and I feel again the need for solitude to get that connection.*

My ego has shaken me up; it tells me too often how crazy I am, unbalanced, etc. – I think such ridiculous thoughts that sometimes scare me – many which include visions of wiping me out. I don't take them too seriously – but I just hear them too often. On the flip side, I've been reading incredible angel stories or miracle tales that give me such ecstatic wonder – life is so mysterious, interwoven with such awe-making mystique that I ponder the layers of reality.

Why do I choose to feel so "victimized?" I certainly have a nice easy life compared to some – I ought to remember that this phase of having youngsters with many demands won't last long. I must not project my disappointments onto Jake. I just feel immobilized at taking control over my life; what I mean is, I seriously want to get an exercise routine going, yet now more than ever I feel unattracted to waking up even ten minutes earlier than necessary. I know working my body would help my mind. I practically detest working so long at a desk too. And then there's the world to reckon with. 2000 have been killed in Colombia by an earthquake, there have been many unusual weather patterns, and we're screwing with DNA whereby a human ear grew on the back of a mouse – shit!

I'm confused as to why it feels impossible to organize my life to meet my needs. I can't figure out how to get the rest I need and still fit in exercise – afternoons are busy with homework time, and evenings are full. If I have some time I always spend it cleaning up clutter. If I don't do something soon I'm worried my body will really go to hell (which is pretty close). So, I have to responsibly deal with stress. I just think, "My God woman, there are so many responsibilities you don't do, look at how dirty your house is! You don't even work forty hours!" Well, at least I don't have problems with physical stuff thank God. I don't do well with those kinds of worries. Counting my blessings helps... Maybe pretend I'm fine and I'll feel fine? I just can't let this pattern persist of feeling overdone.

POETRY SNACK #2

Thank God for the hopping little sparrows
pecking about in the yard
and the bird that tucked itself into the potato vine.
They bring me a teeny bit of cheer
on this sparkling sunny day outside
where there's the deepest gloom inside.

TRAVEL AND TRAVAIL

I loved the Disney movies in which the heroine must trust what's in her heart and follow its messages. Could one go wrong in doing so? It seemed to me that as long as the heart was pure and the thread of Spirit led one forward, a soul could feel safe taking some risks. What my heart was doing now was suddenly directing me to move our family north, away from the city to the small town of Cambria. I couldn't ignore the inner promptings to hightail it to the country. As much as I liked our new home, after four years I was ready to exchange it for a cottage to be closer to the trees and wildlife. Jake was in-between jobs too. Plus, the thrill of taking a risk helped to shift my priorities, dilute my complaints and give me fresh energy. Cambria wasn't far to go but it felt like a huge adventure. I related, *Dear husband that I have, he's more open to going up there, especially since there aren't too many job openings he's come across down here - still, he's not crazy about the idea. My soul seems tormented because I keep "seeing" the change coming, yet I resist rocking everyone's boat. I want God to make it happen if it's for the best, but I also know I have to create what I want.*

I'm wimpy because I have dreams, yet I don't want to cause a huge disturbance. I want Spirit to be involved – I'm afraid of pushing my own agenda too much. It's not like I'll be sad to stay here, in this great custom house with its high ceilings and bullnose corners, with plenty of culture so accessible in town – also, I worry that it's just another one of my crazy ideas persuading me. I recall the whole Charles thing and it makes me look bad! I pray that God will be with me in this drama and not let me get overly forceful in my thought process.

It was an added incentive that my mom, "Nammy," lived in the village being considered. I tired of driving up to visit her, and I wanted to be closer to her should my care be needed. As well, Nammy was the best babysitter! On one particular weekend visit, my mom encouraged me to stop in at a rental agency across from our lunch spot. The planets had lined up perfectly because 1) a fax had just come into the office with a new listing, 2) I was able to see it right away and 3) I fell in love instantly. I felt that God had made it all possible for me to be the first person in line to rent that quaint little cabin in the woods.

What a chore it was for the family to pack up a whole house of too much stuff, but it felt great to pare down beforehand. The timing seemed right. Jake had carpentry to fall back on so we felt pretty secure about the big leap.

The three-bedroom cabin was on a dirt road and nestled in among a ton of pine trees. Just enough sun came through to keep the rosemary and lavender hearty, and to keep the blackberry bushes and poison oak prolific. A miniature plum tree dropped its tiny fruit with loud plunks onto the big deck that went around the back. Raccoons frequently darted across the deck, as did insects and deer, seen from the many windows bearing wobbly old glass and creaky casements. The girls enjoyed climbing huge fallen trees and I adored sitting on the picnic table out on the deck, admiring the view of the wooded canyons beyond. We shared many lovely walks to our mailbox up the road, making up songs about blackberries and bugs. The house itself had so many neat nooks that once when Danya had friends over to play, they played hide and seek twenty-two times! *There are so many moments in my day when I feel deeply and profoundly joyous. The beauty and serenity are tremendous gifts I feel. Once in awhile I fear I have done something ridiculous...Mostly I have the sense that I'm in alignment with my true desire. Jake feels like he is in the Twilight Zone, and it's a lot colder up here. He's so anxious about getting employed. I keep reminding him that God would prefer that he trusts Him.*

My poor husband is being tormented. He seems burdened/ stressed/cheerless – okay, downtrodden. I could have made life so much simpler for him by staying in Santa Barbara. It's hard to feel so happy when he's so miserable. He's disenchanted, not thinking very positively and having limited ideas – it's a difficult period for us both.

Such a pity too that it takes away from his enjoyment of living here. He's staying busy with carpentry but he feels he has to hurry up and get back into the industrial sector or else lose his standing as a manager.

My joyous heart continually leaps - I feel deeply nurtured whenever I look out or step out onto our outdoor space.

Since Jake wasn't thrilled doing carpentry again, he threatened to move the family back to Santa Barbara if he didn't land "proper work" soon. Things had been too easy for me, and I accepted a part-time library job at the girls' school. I told God, *I feel so foolish, and remorseful that I worry about Your plan for Jake. It's so hard to stay up against his discouragement. I hope that his pitiful thoughts aren't creating the continuance of a negative picture. I have a fair amount of guilt about ALL the effort he's expended in sending out resumes.*

We had moved to Cambria in July, but it took until next April for that right job for Jake to come along. Not much time went by before he realized he didn't enjoy commuting those thirty-three miles every day. After nearly a year it seemed logical that we should consider relocating closer to his job. I was okay with switching jobs, rather than commuting myself for the library position that was only ten hours a week.

Once again, I was under the influence of magical timing. As I waited for a clerk in the rental management office, I was guided to look on the blackboard of listings. One of the properties seemed to jump out. I did a drive-by and got that tingly feeling. When an agent walked me through the house later (I was the first to see it this time as well), my soul was doing its singing thing. I detailed, *The right place appeared! I LOVE that feeling when the knowing is strong and instantaneous – when I walked in the door I knew it was to be ours. Once I'd found it I cried from joy and also from wondering how I could be so blessed. Sometimes it seems unfair, yet it's good to love my life. I enjoy my story. Synchronicity is such a pleasure when it's happening.*

When I have moments of quiet relaxation I have a deeply contented feeling, remembering that God really does have the perfect plan and I shouldn't worry. I can trust.

Hauling our possessions back out of the cabin in Cambria proved to be a complete nightmare for the moving guys and us. It may sound unreal, but the house was located at the bottom of twenty-two stairs. Everyone on the job was grouchy with muscle fatigue from carting heavy furniture up those stairs, but delivering the truckload to the cheerful new location in Morro Bay made up for the exhaustion.

Here's what was unbelievable. It wasn't just a dinky house without any character. This charming older home was smack dab across the street from the bay. Not only did we have a stunning view, but we also got to delight in the sounds of the estuary's many residents: cormorants, snowy egrets, herons, gulls, harbor seals, otters, sooty shearwaters and other vagrant species. We viewed sailboat races from the nearby yacht club, and watched kayakers trampling around the dunes on the sandspit. The sunsets were so spectacular that we could hardly break away from the window sometimes.

POETRY SNACK #3

I come to see the sea
I let its blue pureness absolve me
I give to it my surrender
Unresolved conflicts bump about on the white caps
and dissolve into foam
My barge of burdens sails west

◆ ◆ ◆ ◆ ◆ ◆ ◆ ◆ ◆ ◆

The kids didn't seem bothered by another big move, except for the fact that Danya had to go to a new school in seventh grade where she knew not a soul. Dropping her off on her first day that year, I felt terrible remorse. I was Mama Bird who was flinging Baby Bird out into the abyss before I was certain she was ready to fly. It was the kind of disturbance that felt like an emotional bulldozer, and it urged me to overcompensate for a few days. What a relief to see her rapidly adjust without calamity or tears. Having made this move, we now had to drive twenty minutes back to Cambria to visit Nammy, but that ride was a piece of cake: the scenery could not be beat, we were headed for one of our favorite destinations, and it wasn't long enough for the girls to get into a fight!

"D&T" continued to amuse the heck out of Jake and me. *We were listening to a tape with "for he's a jolly good fellow which nobody can deny" – at one point Tessa asked out of the blue, "Mom, what's candy night?"*

I said to Tessa, "Ok, come along love." She replied, "Mommy, I'm not a glove."

One night we were roasting marshmallows at Nammy's out on the deck. It was a very quiet evening. Tessa was amazing herself with her skill of warming the bottom side of her marshmallows. She was so proud of one in particular she loudly declared, "Feel my bottom!" We died laughing!

Tessa fits into a pillowcase so Jake carries her around like a sack of potatoes. She also loves to ride down the stairs in her sleeping bag.

Our little one dubbed the vacuum the "cleaner machiner."

Danya mentioned something about going on strike (since we wouldn't let her eat the melted chocolate we had made for dipping strawberries until after dinner) – and Tessa yelled, "Yeah!" Then she said, "Why did I say that? I don't even know what that means!"

For Pioneer Day at school Tessa wanted to wear a headdress so that she would look like a "tri-bleeder." Oh, she meant tribe leader!

It's cute how Tessa picks up the cat in a childish way. She scoops him up whereby his four paws are all pointing upwards in a furry cluster of kitty feet.

*I had told Tessa she couldn't watch a video until she had eaten her lettuce – she **howled** for an hour!*

Speaking of howling, along came 9-11-01 and I had never bawled so much in my life. I yearned desperately for everything to go back to normal. Life's ordinary stresses were bad enough on people and now every American had to struggle with this great catastrophe. (Peter Jennings did a magnificent job that week.) It was so foreign to my way of thinking that humans could revert to that kind of barbarism. I always used to say the prayer, "God bless everyone and everything," but after 9/11 I gave it up for quite some time. I didn't feel loving enough to pray for the terrorists. My picture of the planet had been drastically altered and I was low on hope. *I do battle with the thoughts that say I ought to be doing some community service or helping somebody, instead of sitting outside enjoying the flowers and the warmth of the lower autumn sun. I just feel insecure and odd. I have ideas to do things like social action and then I negate them, out of despair in a way. I feel mobilized to do something and then decide otherwise.*

9/11 felt like a month-long continual earthquake, shaking up the foundations of what I knew to be safe and rattling any notions of future security. When I wasn't worrying about humanity, I was able to appreciate my pleasurable surroundings. *Heaven is here and now. I hear a songbird twittering and the ocean crashing. I smell the sweet scent of lemon geranium on my hands, and of the other flowers I lovingly planted. I see bright pinks all around me (my gardening palette is simple). The sea air brings me sustenance. The light purple ground cover is abundant and when I park the car I think "Wow" every time. Being here is a big wow all over. Ah, to have the luxury of a few minutes to sit on the front steps and write. It so reminds me of when I journaled at summer camp on the roof.*

Jake and I harbored fear about the world but also about our home being a rental; since it had an incredible location, we worried that the house would soon be put up for sale and that we would be in a pinch to leave. We decided it was time to purchase a house. It was heartbreaking to leave but at least we had a year-and-a-half to experience the wonder of living so close to the bay. Looking back on that period we have admonished ourselves repeatedly for not buying the property, but it was unaffordable at the time. It would end up cursing us – the desire to be near the water has lingered for years, and I think of the curse as our own bittersweet brand of seasickness. I currently still nauseate myself by lusting for a better view, unable to relinquish the desire to own a house that is closer to the water.

We settled for an affordable home in nearby Los Osos with a teeny peek of the bay. Finding this new house didn't go as effortlessly as the previous two had, and I was fairly certain I had looked at one-hundred houses before we made our final choice. (Since then I have had a knee-jerk reaction anytime I see a real estate sign in front of a house; for a second I think, "Ooh, what's this one like?" Just the word "house" is enough to arouse me.) In trying to make the big decision as to which house to buy, the process was physically, mentally and emotionally draining. *Jake and I have had poor relations ever since we've been house hunting. My insomnia has been really bad lately (ok, for years). Part of my problem has been my relentless desire to figure out what we were doing wrong with the house thing – but then I realized how perfect it truly is. I concluded that if I were a character in a story I would want to have faith, trust in the plan and be one who can surrender.*

New house number three had twenty-two rose bushes. With Jake's time and talent we built an extra bedroom in the garage, but still the house became too small and the coming months proved to be challenging. It was apparent that we needed more room, i.e. a more expensive house in which to spread out. In order to obtain the financing, we decided it was finally time to sell the Santa Barbara house that we had been renting out. What I threw into the mix was the idea of moving to New England, since we needed to move again anyway. Nammy had recently moved from Cambria to Maine for the adventure (she loved those summer trips as a young mom to the state so much) and I was still a Yankee at heart. Come every fall I would long to immerse myself in colorful trees and moldy leaf smells, and I heartily missed the architecture of the New England homes and churches, the stone walls, and the exhilaration of the change of seasons. Since I had such good luck with my plans before, I figured, "Why not? We could do it before Danya starts high school. The sale of the house will give us enough to move across country and land a place with a great view and..." La-de-da, dream on girl.

Being the good soul that he was, Jake was open to the possibility of moving back east and could see what I liked about New England. However, he was suffering from adjustment overload. Once the Santa Barbara house sold he began missing "his precious" with fervor. He didn't want to release the object of his imagination and sweat. The house was his own personal creation, like a sculpture, his baby. *It has been hard on Jake. I have regularly found him sitting in our room, staring into space. He's been so full of regret and remorse, as well as anger... I told God I couldn't go thru with the "back east plan." If He had been coaxing me to pursue it, then I have failed in my perseverance. It isn't worth Jake's despair! Nor Danya's. I recognize that my desire for a perfect home helped create a fantasy that wasn't going to be obtained without pain and hardship. I do hate to accept the wide separation Mom and I will experience, but oh well.*

Whatever coaching I offered Jake wasn't enough to help him resurface from his darkness. We needed professional intervention. *Jake will get help with his major self-doubt issues that have been clouding the way he makes decisions. It will be incredible to have him feel more whole... It pisses me off to no end how people in mid-life (such as the two of us) can still have emotionally wrecked parts of themselves that take so much time dealing with. Very irksome!*

True, the ghosts we had hidden were very old remnants from our childhoods. It troubled me how those specters infiltrated my emotional makeup. Jake needed work on his behavior of stuffing his feelings and on facing the neglect he hadn't realized had been haunting him, and I needed to work on "directing traffic" (being pushy). The therapist deemed me as being a classic ACA case (Adult Child of an Alcoholic) since I suffered from insomnia, continual anxiety and other pleasantries. ("Ha! Mere trifles!" I thought.)

Therapy was helping to open those emotional boxes we didn't want to get out, but we knew it was time to start putting our physical stuff into boxes again. Since I had moved often as a kid I supposed it made sense that I moved so much as an adult. Plus, my passion for dollhouses and people houses contributed to my fondness for house shopping. I wondered what our kids would do once they were grown up, and if they would later view our home makeover abilities as good cause for uprooting them all those times.

Our realtor soon told me about something coming on the market, and while I had already seen many appealing selections, the timing of new house number four worked out ideally. Here we go again—I was the first customer to view the house and I was sold on its **potential**, as the current décor bordered on grotesque. There were several kinds of flooring throughout. Much of the inside was painted an unattractive sharp yellow, half of the living room was wallpapered in blue, and the master bath was a hideous bright orange. The kitchen displayed a monstrous mural looking like something out of a doctor's office. Small rocks covered the front and back yards with little else for landscaping. We could see Morro Rock and a little more of the bay and sandspit. Needless to say, the deal went through after I nudged Jake a bit, and we accepted the fact that we would be spending a great deal of time renovating and beautifying. We made a good project team; I had decent success using my intuition to help me in decorating decisions, and he was a good listener who usually deferred to my judgment. Jake especially loved viewing the result of his handiwork after projects were completed. I would forever revere my husband for dedicating his time, skills and creativity to my happiness. WARNING! Laying sod yourself can make you catatonic.

THEN WHAT?

What was going on with our offspring, you might ask? Tessa insisted that we drop the "a" from her name, and Danya's nickname became Donnie. Were the little darlings still darling? Were things harmonious? Danya often nagged Tess, who in turn reacted badly to criticism and slammed doors. Sometimes the sisters had horrific quarrels, many of which centered around which girl would have the honor of sleeping with Miko, the cat. He did not always agree with their plan for alternating nights. Since Miko was Danya's pet originally, she claimed her territory with righteousness. Tess felt it was only fair to share him, and tried coaxing him from his cozy spot on Danya's bed when Tess demanded it was her turn. The situation usually ended up "snaggly" and I would have to pull out my books on discipline and conflict resolution to settle everyone down.

Tess was so boyish in her manner, dress and hairstyle that she was commonly mistaken for a boy, for more than four years! It ended up being a game for Jake and me to see if anyone could properly identify her as a female when our family was out in public. No matter what, anyone who took one look at her referred to her as a he. Luckily this mix-up never bothered her, except for one time in fourth grade when a girl mistook Tess for a boy, and wanted to kick her out of the bathroom at school. Tess's appearance wasn't as much a problem as was her temperament. I wrote in Tess's journal, *I actually don't mind that our daughter wears a shark necklace and a lightsaber™ attached to her belt. It's fine that she plays with super heroes in the tub instead of girly dolls. What I do mind is her lack of sensitivity, her using harsh tones in frequent disagreements, and possessing a bleak outlook when she's tired. Her moods make me question (and want to weep), "Could this be MY child?" I got so annoyed with her once when she was dawdling during teeth brushing, I warned, "I seriously want to inflict flicking on you."*

There were definite benefits to Tess's being a tomboy. Not only had she gotten the rare "outstanding" grade in PE class, she was also a respected soccer player. Her parents affectionately dubbed her "the shark" because of her skill in knowing the sport, driving the ball like mad, shooting gobs of goals and making lovely passes and assists.

It's All in the Way We Play the Game

Being on the outside, it's so easy to judge
Standing on the sidelines I can clearly see where the weak-
nesses are:
bad footing, impulsive kicking, not planning ahead, not paying
attention...
Soccer is surely a metaphor for life
We little people run around chasing things
While we're in the game, we don't see the bigger picture.
Separate players shoot on separate goals, yet
our goals are in fact the same---
to get back to that place
where we are all on one team.

Despite Tess's athletic prowess, she didn't like to fuel her body wisely using fresh vegetables. She would rather chomp on sea salt and bouillon cubes. When we had Danya's friend Fritzi join us one night for dinner, Tess really made me chuckle: *She remarked, "Mom, I think I'm changing. Fritzi's salad actually looks good."* Then one evening when Tess was feeling sick in bed, she mentioned, *I knew that broccoli was toxic.* Even funnier (in a way) was when Jake insisted one night that Tess eat some corn. She sort of pushed a fist into his shoulder. "Use your words," I told her.

She replied breezily, "I'm going to kill you."

"Use your other words," Jake said playfully.

She then said, "I'm going to rip you to pieces."

These comments and interactions bonded us all together as we each made our way through the maze of living and learning within our family unit. The common funny misunderstandings tickled me. Tess had mumbled a comment about sour cream but Danya thought she heard something about the shower curtain! We discovered that "chai tea" got confused with "tai chi" and "tight cheeks." The phrase "warm water" was mistaken for "more modern!" (In high school I loved the mix-up my mom and I had when she asked me for the fly swatter and I brought her ice water.) And there were just plain humorous moments that brightened my day such as, *I jokingly said to Jake, "Oh, now you are being nice to me," and Tess quipped, "Well, you're holding the coffee pot, so what do you expect?!"*

Speaking of jokes, Tess surprised us with this original: What's half of nine cows? Four and a calf! My little jokester totally wins me over by loving the movie <u>The Aristocats</u>. She has seen it more than a dozen times. How could you not adore a child who adores that particular movie? Yet the lighter side of Tess was often balanced by an opposite energy that could pull shadows over my usual upbeat attitude. It was terrific that she got excellent grades in school, but since she displayed the Virgo trait of intensity along with typical pre-teen behaviors, she commonly made scenes more dramatic than necessary. Moodiness was often her "M.O." I always embarrassed her in public, and at home I annoyed her whenever I boogied to music (we're talking a simple movement of the hips). Tess's biorhythm liked to peak at bedtime and she abhorred waking up for school, as her internal clock seemed to be programmed for an 11:00 am wake up time. Just like her mother, Tess couldn't drop off to sleep quickly, and she also suffered from frequent nosebleeds that started unexpectedly. *One night at 3:30 am Tess came into our bedroom crying. I had thought she was having another bad nosebleed. Instead she was suffering from a terrible tummy ache. She was feeling so uncomfortable that she said, "Mom I can't do this. I'm too young to die." Wow, was I alarmed!* After she went to the bathroom and purged the disturbing germs, I was filled with tremendous gratitude and relieved that I could put a halt to my visions of taking her to the hospital. Another night we discovered a way to induce accidental stomach distress and heaving:

for dessert Tess mixed one serving of ice cream with whipped cream and sprinkles, then drank a glass of orange juice and bounced on the bed about twenty-two times. (There's that number again! It is supposed to have cosmic significance, somewhere.)

Since Tess is such a bouncy, energetic person it made sense that she would be attracted to a hyperactive dog. After having attended a summer camp working with dogs at the county shelter, she persuaded us to let her own a dog. Sparky was a high-strung smooth fox terrier with tons of personality. He was the robot dog without an off switch. One fond memory I have of Sparky was finding him on top of the dining table licking leftovers off a plate. Sadly, we took him to the Humane Society after I had a job that required him to be home alone too long. Mia came along later and adjusted well to a quiet home life. She is a sensitive rat terrier that was named after one of Tess's heroes, the famous soccer player Mia Hamm. She is compact and easier to sleep with. She's the mutt-mutt with the cute butt, and should be called a bat terrier because of her tall pointy ears. Mia smells to me just like popcorn or soy sauce-flavored jellybeans. She loves eating used goopy tissues. Her turbo speed typically impresses other dog owners and she often receives comments about her "wheels." The reader should be aware that if you haven't yet raised a puppy, you might not expect that mirrored closet doors can be bitten into, as can garage siding, dirty socks and coffee tables.

On occasion, Mia hunts down my earplugs and she alternates between chewing them into bits and batting them around our bedroom. One evening Tess came into the room to find scattered pieces of blue earplug on the rug and she remarked, "Oh, I see Mia got an earplug... I wonder what she would do with a used Q-tip?" Picturing such a thing, I blurted out a reaction of "Ewwwww, gross!" That dog is trouble. Trouble and nine-tenths. Still, I'm utterly amazed at how, despite having such a small head, she has the brains to know exactly when it's her five o'clock dinnertime! Playing with Mia can be particularly entertaining when Tess gets out the "red laser beam dog exerciser" and I have nearly wet my pants while watching this game in action. Mia tries desperately to catch the red dot that Tess tricks her with, and the dog hunts it like it's a delectable hopping bug that teleports around the room. When I dangle a knotted rope before Mia and she snatches it, my own excitement level rises to where I sound just like Austin Powers saying, "Come on baby, YEAH!"

Big sister Danya turned out to have several artistic talents. She won a number of awards in acrylic painting and other mediums. She loved making her own books, dolls and clay figurines, and also enjoyed altering her own clothes. She and her grandma Nammy spent several creative days building a glorious fairy house. Art aside, Danya is passionate about dancing. She worked her way up through several levels and in her senior year performed as "Clara" in the local Nutcracker. Getting her pointe shoes was a real red-letter day. In academics Danya had excelled in math since middle school and became a tutor throughout high school. Some of her accomplishments could in part be attributed to the fact that she's a Scorpio, for her traits of being meticulous, compulsive and determined proved clear time after time.

Donnie has been drawn to everything Japanese. Jake and I wondered if she might have been Japanese in a former life, for she has shown great interest in Japan's food, music, fashion and culture. We eventually granted her a month in Tokyo to study abroad as a high school graduation gift. It was difficult for us to part with her. In attempting to let go (it had already been so hard watching her drive off to school) I found it necessary to unclog the sinkhole in my heart and let the sorrow drain out into my notebook. The huge adjustment of allowing my baby to be grown up made my heart ache. *I think I'm coming down with something. Or rather, something is about to come up. Maybe it will take the form of a poem. It will center around my having wept tonight, while going through some old pictures of the kids.*

There she was, not a moment ago, being her silly childish self – a child with glasses and braces whom we tucked in at night. Now our first-born is a world traveler with contact lenses and straight teeth who leaves her comfort objects at home.

Here I sit with my popcorn, mixed drink and soggy tissues, telling myself it will be okay. She will find love, she will find truth, and she will share some with us.

The Loss of One Baby

It's already over.
The cap and gown pictures have been sent.
Now she's on a plane to Japan, a lovely girl alone.
Carting hope and dried fruit, goodwill and protein bars,
excitement and host family gifts.
Will her dancer's legs cramp up?

Will she be safe and sound for a whole month?
(Without me?)
She was carried lovingly in my belly
now she's in the belly of that steel bird
being carried away from parental territory
from our caring control
gone for good as she rides out of
childhood into the dawn of her brilliant future.

She's the star of all our nights
The sun in our days
A star up on stage and
Number one for her final grades.

So, baby no more
Woman not yet
Adventures galore? You bet!

We give her to you, Great Mystery
Only you get to keep her now.

In any case, that high-need baby paddled her way to the top of
her class, gave the Valedictorian speech at graduation and is now

enrolled with a nice scholarship at Stanford University. (She is a better writer than I.)

A few little funnies I noted in Danya's journal from her pre-college days were: *She offered to make muffins and insisted I not help her. I had left a can of Pledge™ on the counter since I had more dusting to do. Danya inadvertently sprayed the muffin tins with the Pledge™ and not the butter spray!!!*

While driving up to Canada we let Danya practice driving. After her hour was up Jake exclaimed that he needed cigarettes and some new underwear! [He doesn't smoke.]

Danya had walked into our room and saw Dad naked coming out of the shower – it made her hiccups go away!

The very day she left for college, I was a mess. Writing helped me address the feelings of loss that had returned.

There She Goes Again

I feel a poem brewing.
It starts with a feeling of restlessness.
What is it my soul is whispering?

There is sadness down deep.
Percolating fear.
Bubbles of worry coming to the surface.
What advice am I neglecting to tell the child I must let go?
What guidance am I forgetting?
I pray for her protection and know this is a better use of time.
Yet there are too many what-ifs that impart shadows. I'm afraid of failing her.

I turn to the bright side – she wants to go,
And she looks forward to coming back home.

Oh Danya my dear
I'm often racked with fear
Into the world you are propelled
And I am thus compelled
To worry

My Fear and Worry List
has grown longer having become a mother
having seen what the world can unleash
spiders are fine, but what scares me are:
major dental work
MS
rapists
speed (roller coasters, driving over 75mph, skiing)
Lyme Disease
child molesters
nuclear war/terrorism
getting bald spots in old age

Danya came home a vegan after her first year at college, and I have enjoyed preparing most of her dinner menu suggestions. Perhaps her most interesting dessert selection we have tasted to date has been her homemade kale and tofu mint ice cream. Let me just say that kale farts smell a lot worse than asparagus pee. Think how appalling it would be if, in old age, I had forgotten all about that wonderful ice cream, provided I hadn't typed it up here already.

I definitely like Danya's arrivals. She always heads straight for the pantry, fridge and freezer where she compulsively organizes everything in them. I do not like her goings so much. Knowing she would be leaving again tomorrow for another school year made my body feel poorly. I caught myself staring into space a few times, numb, my eyes glazed over——I was either really under the weather, or suffering early from the effects of her departure. I felt like a flower might, at the moment that its petals drop off and blow away.

Collage

The clutter on my desk forms a mosaic
a snapshot of my life at this unique time,
the group of odd objects creating a freeze-frame
from an average day
        an anniversary photo
        ignored paperwork
        an earplug kept away from the dog
        pieces of poems to be
        my daughter's handmade pincushion from school
        notes that came to mind at 1:00 am
        a reminder to clean the rug

Simple things spread before me
small bits of chaos
the preoccupations of a mother
filler to help me avoid being quiet and still

The draw of the outer world captures and captivates me
It is the standard lens I use
but, at times, I see broken barriers,
where I can focus on the brilliant

Author's Note: My chronological story is hereby finished at this point.
The following sections are the ramblings (past and present) of a person
who enjoys scribbling out thoughts haphazardly for her own amusement, and hopefully for yours to some degree.

ADDENDUM

Holiday Hyper

Christmas is my favorite time of the year. I'm an all-out Christmas fanatic, and should probably own a bumper sticker that says, "I brake for Christmas decorations." I'm obsessed with seeing every little festive ornament that I can, inside and out, and simply can't get enough of the holiday fanfare. I even make my family sit through unbearably bad holiday movies, just so I can fulfill that urge to squeeze in as much Christmas merriment as possible. During these days of dazzle I see myself as a spongy spinning top, bent on absorbing all of the gaiety, and whirling in all directions so I don't miss anything pretty. This fascination can be attributed to the fact that my mother has got Christmas down. Except for the year she got divorced, there was never a time in my life when she didn't make this holiday incredibly special. An early childhood memory that stands out is when I received a dollhouse with lamps that lit up and a doorbell that rang. That thing won first place as far as Christmas presents go. In other years Mom made hand-sewn dolls, doll clothes and blankets. She would always find the best things too and wrap them so handsomely. I didn't inherit her ability to fashion terrific bows; maybe it's because I'm left-handed, which handicapped me in learning how to sew.

At Christmas I love the contrast between the dark outside and the twinkly light inside. I adore the music and the spirit of love behind everything. How lucky I am that my dear neighbor Judy shares this fanaticism with me. She decorates early and has an abundance of joy to share with me, and we giggle from Christmas enthusiasm like kindergarteners. Come January, I grieve over the removal of our decorations, especially that of our tree. I find it wrenchingly difficult to part with it – its woodland perfume, its brilliant cheerfulness, its earthy majestic presence – I feel such loss when it is gone. Tess even commented, "I don't like the hole that it leaves behind. It's so empty." Before I let Jake take the tree outside this year, I needed to inhale as much of the sweet fragrance as I could. I gently grabbed many of its branches, noticing how soft most of the needles still were, and I thanked it for giving me so much pleasure.

With every year at Christmas there is an ache inside that's a calling to lead me to a private place—at best in snow somewhere—but most importantly away from loads of people and the exchange of gifts (when ill-selected on the other end are embarrassing), and the lack of devotion and thanks to God. Of course another part of me thinks it's all an expression of God no matter where I am and what I'm doing—but if my choice, I would prefer a quiet intimate celebration, a time of reverence, joy, peace and less driving!

As we did not get to a church tonight, I wish to bring church into my heart. I long for that rich feeling to fill my being, I yearn to be lifted up to higher thought and greater peace. I want to connect with that spirit of total love and joy and release. In all reality I don't need to have the candles and music and stir of excitement, for it is all here with me, available at every moment.

Cursed with PMS and Not Sleeping

A few years ago I developed this theory that when premature babies are adults they don't sleep as well as other people. I was simply shocked when my doctor concurred last week that I was right! I figured that there had to be some correlation between being separated from your mother as an early newborn and then being uncomfortable in bed as a grown-up. My doctor said that premies have an underdeveloped nervous system and can be more sensitive to touch. No wonder I don't like having Jake touch any part of my body when I want to sleep. My neurons, not being fully encased, may contribute to my need for making constant adjustments to my nightgown, hair, pillow, underwear, sheet and blanket to feel "right." Added to my list of irritants, if the sheet touches my earplug it makes a loud scraping sound in my ears, necessitating one more adjustment. Accompanying these obstacles to my falling asleep are the misfortunes of having a weak bladder, sensitive hearing and over-stimulated brain.

When I have PMS, my negative thoughts gunk up my brain and it feels like pulling taffy to get them out. There are times at night when a haze of cloudy restless thoughts penetrates any peacefulness I was trying to achieve, as if an electric storm were buzzing very dimly but with irksome tirelessness. Even the most mundane thoughts swirl around and repeat themselves over and over and their stickiness whips up a mental tornado that is hard to ignore.

I can remember a few years back when there would be nights I would dread going to bed. It's happening again, long stretches where sleep is a difficulty and my fidgeting body and rambling mind can't get easily comfortable. I feel ashamed at having this problem, at cussing more frequently (mostly to myself inside), at feeling like a failure and having fuzzy thinking / poor memory.

A typical night during the two weeks that I have PMS is getting up to pee four or five times, whether I drink anything in the evening or not. Once I woke up three nights in a row at 3:00 am. I have tried different mental exercises to outsmart my body but my bladder is a weak holding tank. I can visualize up the wazoo and it does nothing to prevent the urge to go. So not only do I act like the girl in <u>The Princess and the Pea</u> because of how easily disturbed I am in bed, you could also say that I am incensed by the pee! (And I am cheated out of my chi.) In my exhaustion I've even thought briefly about sleeping in the bathroom, but since we have one of those smaller California homes with teensy water closet rooms, I wouldn't be able to stretch out at all. One of the most unsettling times was when I was asleep for a whole ten minutes and then the cat woke me up by pushing our door open. Next, I got up to pee four times. Jake was snoring loudly due to congestion. I wasn't able to find my earplug that was usually in its regular spot under my pillow, and I was too tired to get up for another one. The cat started crying at 4:45 am and at 5:30 I finally got up to feed him.

Those pre-dawn hours when I'm up and down make me feel like a phantom. I rise from my warm bed and use the king of swear words more than once, plodding back and forth to the bathroom. The prospect of waking up to the alarm becomes progressively grim as the hours wear on. At least I've adapted to my condition over the years and no longer feel sick in the morning from not sleeping well.

It doesn't help that I allow my mind to create "fear fantasies." Sometimes I obsess about scary thoughts and I've become good at making up ghastly stories. I know of other mothers who have joined the same "club"; they too imagine all the awful things that could happen to their families. One mom who shared her scary fears with me had to live through her own nightmare when her young husband collapsed and died while playing in a baseball game. Changing the channel in my head isn't always easy since the grip these images have on me is glue-tight. My sensitive nature cannot even handle listening to the news, reading the paper or watching many PG-13 movies, for their details and graphic images feed my fear. If I hear a story about women and children being murdered in Baghdad I'm emotionally wounded for days. Or take the cases of the boys who inhaled a deadly parasite while swimming in a lake and died within two weeks. The insecure side of me uses these stories as evidence that the world is dark and I am a potential victim.

One saving grace I have found, thanks to the advice given by Paramahansa Yogananda, is to immediately and silently proclaim, "I don't want that to be created." As soon as I hear myself drumming up a frightening mental picture, I try to steal that output with a "No, you come back here" and snatch it out of the universe. This mantra has been my regular lifesaver and has shown me that I can limit the negative energy my ego wants to snipe at me. Still, I am amazed at how often I hear that voice of doom in the caverns of my mind. If my kid has ridden her bike to a friend's, I become afraid she will get in an accident. If my other daughter has driven into town with buddies during a storm, I think the worst and worry about their safety. I used to think that my mother was abnormally concerned about the welfare of her loved ones, but now I see that her worry arose from fears that were just as pernicious as mine. When I can free myself from the trappings of my wily ego, I can let God work in me like Bob the Builder™--He can fix it, yes He can! When I don't surrender, I keep myself awake longer. Thoughts fly around in my head aimlessly and repeatedly, like the way those 3-D text phrases skirt endlessly across a computer monitor in the old simplified screen savers. My mind darts about like a spider making its web. I pull at thoughts just as the spider tugs and tucks its threads, weaving rows in and out. I snatch a thought here, grab an idea there, and the web gets sticky with clutter. One evening I knew I had to work harder to free myself from thinking, and tried conjuring peaceful imagery to help me fall asleep. I pictured myself alone in the late summer sun, lying on a dock in a lake with a hat over my face. The temperature was perfect and the dock bobbed gently. The air smelled wonderfully sweet. No one was near to ask things of me; having a good hour of quiet ahead of me calmed me considerably, and I was ready to rest amid the tranquil scenery. Suddenly my mind yanked out a disturbing question, and my unsettled musing acted like a loud motorboat that sped by, sending a large wake that crashed into my reverie. I was a spider stuck in her own web.

Some nights it is so hard to get to sleep and I shift positions in bed a good fifteen times. Some days the nuisance of PMS hovers over me in an annoying way, just as the blackbird relentlessly torments the crow by harassing it, not leaving it alone. On other days PMS is a fierce and nasty demon. It makes me overreact and feel miserable. Jake made a comment that I let hurt my feelings, and on top of that, Tess's complaints helped form a pit I jumped into: that place where I feel I'm letting her down. She is so good at letting storms blow over quickly and I'm awful at not letting the upset go; our conflicts can bother me for a few hours. What's funny is I'm probably caring more about her happiness than I need to. Remembering that I'm choosing to act this way brings me back to sanity, but there are moments when I do really want to run away.

Jake's snoring makes a wide variety of different sounds. I joke to myself, he snoreth like a mockingbird singeth. Tonight his snoring commenced like the puffing sound of a locomotive taking off. Then the whistling that his nose made sounded like our dog was whimpering. I wish I didn't have such a keen sense of hearing. My powers of obser-rvation, particularly listening, could make me a good detective. There aren't many noises that escape me. Even small creaks wake me up. I can hear the foghorn quite easily and Jake claims it's been inaudible to him for nearly a year. Ignoring the racket my belly sometimes makes is difficult when it sounds like a thunderstorm, complete with crackle, pause and boom. I wear just one earplug because I'm afraid of being totally cut off from the world when I wear a pair, and the sound I hear in my head when I wear the earplug sometimes makes me think that it's raining inside my pillow.

Not only do external sounds disturb my nights but I am also affected by the music in my head. When God created me, he hotwired an iPod™ into my brain. It usually turns on automatically right at bedtime when I'm PMSing, and will not shut off for what seems like hours. The volume might be low but it always plays over and over. I've either unwittingly tuned into my choir music or the jumpy rock tunes that my younger daughter adores.

Daytime PMS is a lesser nuisance, as I have more control over my edgy thoughts then than at night, but that's not saying much. Little things still become huge annoyances; accidentally letting my apron strings dangle into the toilet bugs the hell out of me, and there always seem to be more than the normal amounts of curly pubes on the bathroom floor and they make me cringe. Dust is even dustier and appears insurmountable. I especially irritate myself if I say something twice like, "Mia, you want your treat now? You want your treat now, girl?" Even contemplating the things I need to take care of puts undue stress on me and I feel caged in; if two topics come to mind, that number seems to explode, and in overreacting I feel there is too much pressure and I cannot succeed. PMS is oppressive, and it subverts logical thought.

On no it's back again. The PMS shroud felt so tangible – I knew I was under its spell once more. After feeling displaced for an hour I got a grip, acknowledging that people in truly wretched health were still able to think positively and improve their conditions – so taking the path of affirmations made a difference.

Sometimes I feel so tired that I develop an instant envy for those people who can go right to sleep on airplanes. How do they shut down and conk out so quickly?

An Exaggeration, Mostly

There once was a lady called K
Whose husband kept her sleep at bay
With his regular snoring
From night until morning
And poor K was tired all day.

Life is a Metronome

Tick tock
my body is a clock
As I drag myself to the bathroom at night
every two hours
I feel its tiresome rhythm in every step
in and out of bed
I consider how springy my step is, come mid-morning time

In and out
up and down, the image of our perfectly split world
It is the constant beat of the universe
It is the infinite play of being born and dying
It is why my soul needs to hear the ocean breathe

Seedpods burst forth into the soil, powered by their own
fireworks
Black holes are swallowed and disappear

A child struggles against its independence
then flourishes as it flies free

Drought and floods
inspiration and despair
contentment and self-loathing
We try to balance on life's teeter-totter
straddling the current
crossing the stream on a fallen log that was someone's helping
hand
or slipping, falling in
perhaps jumping – to surrender the boundaries

The edges are colored in forcefully
We can blend like crayons and melt into the seams
finding the perfection we seek
right down the middle
where the halves collide.

Mockingbird and Me

I'm sure there are others who are awake at this hour
2:30 am
breastfeeding mothers
college kids
truck drivers and postal workers
bakers just now arising

but here in the crazy room of Insomnia Land
I'm only aware of the mockingbird singing from the pole in the
street
He makes it pleasant for dozing when it's intermittently
possible
I notice his cheerful tunes when I'm not fixated on my
discomfort.

I really didn't want to get up and write this.

May my dreary thoughts rise like the bakers' bread.

The Soft Voice of Reason

I am the kind of person who loves getting messages. Not phone messages, but rather those that are relayed from the universe. They are communications I receive thankfully, although I frequently do not pass the information onto my brain. I am coached and guided by a Voice without a body, a Voice so quiet that I sometimes barely register its direction. It matters not whether the Voice is my internal teacher, higher self or courier from the beyond; I only know that it always serves me well. Missing its helpful hints and clues isn't always problematic, like when I need aid with a simple kitchen appliance – but had I not heeded its warnings in the case of a pending traffic accident, the result would have been life-threatening.

There was no doubt I heard "Wait!" in my head just before I was about to turn onto the highway during my green light. I stopped, just when a motorist ran through their red light. That particular example proved to be the greatest benefit and relief I can call to mind, but there are copious examples of my "being saved" by the Voice for years. Sometimes I distinguish the Voice as coming from an invisible angel next to me, and at other times I sense it residing inside me as a firm knowing. I'm convinced that angels exist. I have a good friend who can see them in her house, as can her daughter.

A few moments ago my Spirit helper advised me to find our missing checkbook in the back of the truck. Naturally I had spent a good bit of time searching for it first, often looking in the same places twice (how infuriating!) and certainly becoming more concerned by its lack of appearance anywhere I tried. Perhaps I just got lucky, or perhaps the Voice waited until I reminded myself not to freak out – that it would turn up once I quieted down. Thank goodness it did. I was so grateful I didn't have to call the bank.

The Voice gives me all kinds of comforts and smaller alerts. Our cat was very ill recently, and I felt drawn to hold him despite his condition. I heard, "Rock him like you used to, as this may be the last time." Later that evening the Voice predicted, "Here comes Danya telling us he's died." That was exactly what happened a minute later. She opened our bedroom door fraught with grief that he had just passed.

It's incredible how many countless times I have been coached by the Voice, and how many times I have neglected it. One day while going out to the garden, I went to put on one of my slip-on shoes. The Voice said, "Hold it, you should check it first." My reaction was to ignore the warning – of course there would be nothing in my shoe. As soon as I slipped my foot in, I felt something cold and slimy. There was a little baby frog in the toe of my shoe! I was so worried I had hurt him, but he seemed just fine and let me move him safely to our fountain. At least I hadn't shoved my foot in. I'm always amazed at the audacity I display when I don't heed the cautions of the Voice.

Shortly after the frog episode the Voice was suggesting that I not let Danya take her car into town, as "something might happen." My response was, "Nah, it's been working fine." Never argue with Spirit! (If that's what the Voice is.) Yes, the car broke down after she got to town, yes I felt stupid and yes, I could have saved myself three hours of dealing with the tow truck, the car shop and waiting for a ride.

You might think that due to the frequency with which I observe the Voice giving me a hand, I would be more prone to giving it my full allegiance. Unfortunately my ego much prefers that it be in charge and thinks it knows best. There have been hundreds of times when I didn't tune in or I blatantly disregarded guidance, and then always regretted my foolishness. Those decisions to choose my own will occurred within nanoseconds, but most of the time I could pinpoint that instant when I heard the Voice and thought, "Nah..." There were moments though when I was obedient and did remember that its wise messages would save my ass.

A comfort that comes from my connection with this helping from Spirit is the sense of utter completeness it brings. When everything "lines up" there is a cheery serendipity that is so fulfilling. The Voice will tell me, "Yes, this is the house for you." "That's YOUR job." "Yes your kid will get accepted to that college." Other times I have a keen knowing that surprises me. The phone might ring and instantly I will know who it is before answering it. The Voice can be remarkably faint, but when these statements are fed to my brain and I do pay attention, there is a spine-tingle that makes my body know that it is truth. Spirit is magic and majestic, and I get a glow when I KNOW.

Observations from Middle Age

Now that I have crossed the half-life mark and I'm in my autumn years, my upper lip is withering badly. I see how the skin on my forearms buckles up like a carpet. When I'm bent over, my belly hangs down like a very old puckered orange. My chin hair requires more management and I should probably get it waxed. This particular curse should befall men since facial hair is **their** domain!

Having snakeskin and the baggy sock look around my calves makes me realize that I simply inhabit my body as a turtle in a shell does, because I still feel young inside even though I'm decaying slowly on the outside. As humans we are akin to the leaves of the baby scrub oak --- soft and tender at a young age, but then with time we become pointed and prickly at the edges.

Daily I watch the fissure in my face deepen as time speeds on. It is an ugly widening wrinkle above my lip that serves as a mark of my undeniable maturity, and it feels absolutely absurd to be this old already. I worry about the crack getting deeper so I try to remember not to whistle, for fear that getting my mouth into that shape will make the line worse.

As the decline of my body continues to hasten, my memory seems to lag behind from the flow of daily events. I seem to have less concentration and am not as sharp as I used to be. Poor Tess often needs to tell me things more than once; am I not retaining data because of old fuses, over-stimulation or a lack of interest?

Different things in my body are making new noises. My gurgling stomach will occasionally sound exactly like the spinning of a toilet paper roll on its holder. During lovemaking the body parts that I always thought should be silent are now making squishy slurpy sounds like the sucking of mud out of a pipe.

For so many years I idealized old age womanhood for the wisdom that it presumably entailed. How late does that wisdom start to kick in?

We live in these body suits for just a short while
What we see from them is a mixed bag
The glorious wonders of flowers, birth, miracles and tenderness
But then the horrors we can view are intense and immense
Too awful for words, too unkind are some of our species.

As the cargo of pitiful memories never really lightens,
many will doff their fleshy carrying cases expeditiously
in exchange for a faster flight beyond. They pop out of this
world disbursing pain to those behind. One heavy suitcase
passes on.

We lumber under not only our possession of things
but also our collection of mental paperweights.
We cosmic travelers should remember that we board that
skyway to Heaven together.

Something about death

Hearing the news of a colossal disaster in the world or of a loved one's pending fatal illness, I feel like a slowly sinking submarine. The dark waters swirl over me as I submerse myself in tragedy's tide. I remember one time it hit me, the time it had all felt so perfect a moment before. The rain rapped gently on the skylights, the crackling embers warmed the room, the candles exuded a nice perfume, the glowing Christmas tree blinked merrily, and the cat switched on its happy motor on top of my tummy. Then Jake informed me of the terrible tsunami that had killed 100,000 near Indonesia. I no longer chose to enjoy the comfort around me. I sank into grief for the dead.

There is the theory or philosophy that people choose their own death. I readily accept this idea in particular cases, as when a person dies peacefully from old age. Some people pick more dramatic ways to die, like driving drunk and crashing. However, when a young child develops a life-threatening illness, a huge catastrophe strikes, or a middle-aged family member is diagnosed with cancer, my response is one of anguish.

Such was the experience for Susan, one of my favorite relatives with the best sense of humor. I can't imagine what it must be like to live with the news that you won't live much longer. She lost her battle at only fifty-six. I hope that Susan felt she had one hell of a ride, and I wish the same for other people who have died young. Rattled also by the untimely death of Heath Ledger, I contemplated,

He will never wake again.
On his last day, what were his first thoughts? Did his mind instantly drop into a character he was rehearsing? Did he picture his child, then his agent?
How we all weep to be robbed of his face.

Although many of us have floated down that tunnel into another world several times already, we hate to picture him traveling there so soon.

He has left behind a former lover who grieves deeply – missing his perfect hug, those glances that only he had given during their glory days. Trapped in her galaxy of despair she is still programmed to listen for his voice, smell his scent, feel his hands. Now she must endure alone, still yearning to reset reality so that they could share in life's discoveries together.

She wants only him, and all the well wishing she receives from a hundred callers makes it hurt all the more to have lost him.

In the wake of his sudden departure we have been reminded again to commit to the moment with passion.

Thinking about how Susan and Heath's lives ended so prematurely makes me question once again my purpose, redetermine my goals, and admit that I don't have a clue what this is all about. Will my accomplishments have meant anything when I die?

Dear God, am I EVER grateful that I have written so much of my life down! The stories and details are RICH! It would have been a huge loss not to be able to go back and read about our babies' births, for instance.

In typing up notes for this book, I sometimes doubted myself and questioned my efforts, and would catch myself looking over at the dog sleeping serenely, as if I could obtain instant clarification from her about what I was doing. Inwardly I posed the question, "Mia, does this really make sense? Will anyone care about these words of mine?" I alternated between thinking my writing was utter rubbish and then maybe one notch above satisfactory. But above all, I felt driven to finish this project regardless of how it would be received, and felt with great seriousness that I had to mark it off my to-do list as one lasting legacy for my kids. Fearing that I could be tragically snuffed any day made me push even harder, and the passing of loved ones always reminded me to treat every day as special.

Bill and His Empty Shoes

Uncle Bill left us today
He packed his bag in a hurry (the lingering shell of his body)
Already the essentials were stowed, but he gathered the rest of his belongings urgently (his final breaths),
off to catch the best sunset ever, traveling down that road to infinite heaven
leaving behind blood, bone and yesterday's shoes –
those that carried their master in pain but are now at rest.

We will miss the gift of your wonderful smile, Bill
You did make the world a better place
No one could ever follow in your shoes

In the end, our lives are zipped up into one miniscule microchip
one lifetime programmed with lesson after lesson
necessary for the next go-round

A kernel of summation
rich with yesterday's joys

full of the cycles of things

Yet its meaning is preserved by few
The marks we make are scattered by the tempests of time
Our names fade like old parchment

Still, it is good to walk this earth awhile.

Random Meanderings

Smelling is big on my list of great things to do and it gives me data about my past and present world. I like how fragrances connect me to other people. This morning on my walk to the bay I noticed wafts of sweet alyssum, men's cologne, burnt toast and canoe varnish, and I enjoyed picturing the faces associated with these whiffs—the old lady gardener, the businessman, the mom running late and the retired gentleman. Sniffing patchouli on someone at the farmers' market makes me relive my hippie days for a second and I am reminded of free-spirited youthfulness. Catching the aroma of bacon and waffles at my neighbors' house helps me imagine them sharing a relaxed and cozy scene. The smell of Asian noodles from the house on the corner gives me an instant image of the thin man who lives there, and how I always see him walking back from town laden with grocery bags. Skunks bring the wilderness creatures directly into my awareness, and coffee brewing inside a bookstore is the ultimate heavenly blend of liquid and written inspiration. I also love how certain smells trigger memories, and when they pop up I return to those moments with vivid recall--unless the smell attaches itself to a memory so slippery that it eludes me, and the setting from the past does not materialize.

Maybe I'm like you. Some of my favorite smells are coffee beans, vanilla, Christmas trees and warm pine needles, tomato vines, freshly mowed grass, lavender, Mr. Lincoln roses, and the baby aisle at the grocery store.

Like the skunks, there are those awful odors we experience, the old beer and nasty subway smells. Perhaps you are familiar with that stinky spot cleaner called Resolve™. One day I thought I smelled it in the house. I asked Jake if he had used it to clean up some cat barf or something. He just laughed! I wondered why on earth he found something humorous in that question. It turned out he had just sprayed on some eucalyptus cologne that he had wanted me to give a second try. Previously I said it smelled yucky, and he had disagreed with me. The cologne really did smell like a cleaning agent!

◆◆◆◆◆◆◆◆

With regard to dreams, I am intrigued by those dreams that dissolve, whose shadows slip away before the mind can pinch a piece of their remembrance. How are their messages heard, their imprint felt, their impact received? I am told the subconscious does file dream information away, but I wonder how the smoky smudgy dreams compare with the ones that burn their impression into you. It's fascinating to come out of a deep dream and feel like you are slowly swimming to the surface from the bottom of a very big pool.

Recently I woke up surprised. I dreamt that I was a student at Stanford and that I ran into my old friend Alison from high school. Despite my amazement at dreaming I was attending college, I was delirious with joy to see her again! (And pleased that we both turned out so smart.) Thirty years have passed but I still miss the friendship we shared. She rejected me as a friend back in 1980 after I told her about the ashram I attended. I find it curious that I haven't let go of that disappointment. Perhaps my nostalgia makes me miss her the same way my mom misses her mother's fried chicken, collard greens, biscuits and homemade peach ice cream. We want to recapture those memorable moments and linger there.

This morning I had an unusual dream about life – it was where you could take an image and mix it with sea and sky and everything would blend together. Just like how God is in all the seams. The lines would blur and you could see how we are all the same and come from the infinite universe.

I wonder how we each use the blurriness to our advantage – what we do to blot away our iniquities like in a watercolor. We can dab here and there at our denials, smooth over the bumpy splotches, or, even sneakier, water down our outrages.

◆◆◆◆◆◆◆

I couldn't remember if it had been four or five days since my husband and I had sex (I usually kept track pretty well, for his sake). I was sad that we weren't lining up like the planets do. Rather, it felt as if we were two people careening through space, bombarding each other now and then. I ignored how he had the exact same look on his face as the dog did – that of quiet begging. Suddenly though, my inner axis shifted ever so slightly and it seemed like the world looked larger. Life had opened up to reveal what the wide-angle lens held in waiting while I had been resisting the grander view. I had spent manifold moments fighting the Spirit's call to love – punch, pow, WHAM. As things shifted and my heart cracked open again, I could glimpse the instant of fulfillment whereby love moved more deeply inside me, and I saw my husband in a renewed way. I hoped that this inspiration would grace my life through old age.

♦ ♦ ♦ ♦ ♦ ♦ ♦

On a recent trip I noticed I was instantly drawn to a man who was writing in a notebook at Starbucks and then to a man writing in a journal on the café car of the train. It made me feel like starting a writing party right there and then. But seeing as how I am made up of so much self-doubt, I reasoned that just because I write doesn't mean I'm any good at it. I fear I don't live up to a certain expectation about writers, undelineated as it may be in my mind. Plus I battle with having two sides to me: one that is content to be out walking the dog and being the busy mom, and the other that wants only to sit alone and write.

The urge to write comes upon me now but after several minutes I haven't found an interesting subject to address. Perhaps it would be wise for me to simply write for nothing but pleasure.

I can't think of anything finer than to have this blessed quiet time to myself (I'm currently unemployed), where I can sit and admire the roses, dianthus, lavender and sea thrift which paint my world beautiful. I can watch the clouds invade the bright summery day, be touched by the sea breezes, hear gorgeous classical pieces on MY radio station and recklessly throw the dog's toys to her. These joys are so minor but so appreciated. I enjoy taking time out to open and expand my thinking, and to pay attention to what I may have been missing.

I like how putting my pen to the notebook is a loving walk inside. Pondering the temporarily blank page makes me think, "What's up? What's next? What's in my heart?" The quest within is always a success.

◆◆◆◆◆◆◆

Looking back at itty-bitty snippets from my life, I can always see the universal theme of duality in so many moments. I see myself as the perfectly happy child, spending delightful hours with my Liddle Kiddles™ dolls or my kiddy kitchen set in the closet, or dancing merrily around the coffee table to the opening theme of "The Monkees" TV show. Then I can also view the rewind of the hurt and frustration, the agony of having a brother who let his friend blow a tack into my leg, and the anxiety of a pending parental argument. Yin-yang's pendulum swings irregularly nowadays when I notice I fall in and out of love with my husband. Love's grace sometimes wanes, based on the frequency of certain bad habits like his tossing toenails haphazardly towards the trash can, leaving damp towels from the fish tank on the kitchen table, and blowing his nose in the shower. I also get annoyed at how he sucks at his teeth trying to clean them and it sounds just like a mini bug zapper. It's obvious that the selective perception that comes with new love and early romance fades with the years, and that spouses must be vigilant at keeping their relationship healthy (i.e., airing grievances verbally, or flaunting them in one's book). But what a great guy! Here's a man who spent a whole weekend painting our neighbor's house because it was such a hideous blight on the neighborhood. Then we must factor in Jake's tenderness and how it touches me deeply, particularly regarding his affection for his daughters, and I find him utterly endearing. Jake enjoys being frisky with the girls and one of his favorite retorts is, "I've had enough of your guff, Miss McGruff." He impresses me with his wit, intelligence and playfulness. Even his love of fish is adorable. His aquatic pets do little for me, but the passion he feels for them deserves appreciation.

I love watching good comedies with Jake when he repeatedly booms in laughter and slaps his knee. Better still, my adoration increases when he tears up from a scene that moves his heart. He is my hero, and we are lucky to be together, blessed to share this cog on the wheel of life. Yet, I must admit how terrible I feel that I do kiss the dog more than I kiss him. Well, she's home more than he is.

Another example of a dichotomy that I find intriguing is my refusal to catch the white moths that are terrorizing our garden, and yet I have no reservations about catapulting snails over the fence. I enjoy other contradictions, like the interior decorator who lives with old wallpaper borders of hearts and bears (how outdated!), the psychiatrist who is married to the abuser of prescription drugs, the colorblind botanist who names a plant for a color it isn't (i.e. the blue dick flower is purple), and the gorgeous rose bushes that grow bountifully in a yard filled with junk cars and lots of trash.

◆◆◆◆◆◆◆

It's fun to consider how common sounds can misrepresent themselves. Once I heard two doves alighting from the phone wire and the noise they made sounded just like a horse whinnying. Sometimes birds sound like dangling dog collars, and barking dogs can sound like otters. The eucalyptus trees scraping together squeak like an automatic garage door opener. The brant geese often make a funny tone that is even more garbled than gargling. Certain sounds I **really** like, such as sacred choral music, can transport me to the outer galaxies. I must have been a nun in a former life because usually when I listen to chants, pieces by classical composers and many other works, I am lifted into the heavens while being rooted deeply inside my heart. Sometimes I can barely drive because I'm tearing up from a particularly gorgeous musical creation. My brother's musical creations set off sparks in my heart, along with a small amount of jealousy, because of the way he strings notes together like exquisite poetry.

Getting to sing classical pieces is a similar story because it is an instant blast-off into heavenly space. I openly thank God for giving me a decent singing voice so I can enjoy the rapture of performing in a chorale. A moment of intoxication arrives for me when I've learned my music pretty well and I can begin really hearing the magnificent blend of all the parts, the different harmonies coloring each composition. To me, the tones coming from a choir are cleaner and purer than the dramatic, forced throaty groan sounds heard from someone auditioning for "American Idol." It's such a heart-opening experience in choir rehearsal at times, especially when we work on Christmas music. Once, when I was placed next to a tenor in rehearsal, I felt that our connection wasn't just in vocal harmony. It was also a tandem soul encounter as well. We became spontaneous spiritual siblings in a chorus of angelic voices.

Being a singer who loves to write (or a writer who loves to sing) can have corresponding complications. Song after song, or one tune hashed over repeatedly, either blocks out or competes with my inner word processor for brain time. It is nearly impossible to get to sleep after an energizing rehearsal.

In fact, music plays in my mind to such an extent that I can hear strains of imaginary notes playing throughout our home's heating vents. I think I'm picking up a melody somewhere when really I'm just unintentionally making it up. Perhaps it's similar to the way I enjoy finding faces or profiles among walls, floors and towels when I'm in the bathroom. It's such a fun game to seek any little face hiding in the tile and cement. I trick myself into thinking that it's the "artist's eye" I'm putting to use, but it's probably because one more little screw has become loose in my noggin.

♦♦♦♦♦♦♦♦

I thought for a moment it had finally left me; when I turned my New England calendar to October this year, I wasn't hit with my usual "autumn lust". I obviously hadn't taken a moment to think about what I was missing. As soon as I began to remember, the ache returned. After all these years, I still cannot avoid that pressing desire to immerse myself in the fall colors of nature. I carry a nagging craving to take walks in the cool air, with a canopy of bright branches overhead, while crunching on crispy leaves bedded underneath boots, and insisting that my family inhale the glorious woody perfume---but that setting doesn't exist while we live. You might think I had adjusted by now.

Having left New England at age nineteen, and then later relocating from the Midwest to central California, I endured nearly twenty-five subsequent years of longing for autumn's delightful gifts. To help offset what I was missing, I would drive five hours north to throw myself into Yosemite's spectacular beauty; yet it wasn't Vermont with its cabins and wood smoke, and it didn't have charming roadside shops. Neither did it have one of my very favorite things: stone walls. Or barns or ancient cemeteries. While visiting nearby local towns in the fall, whenever I spied a pretty tree with colorful leaves up ahead I would slow down, take a mental photograph and try to absorb the tree's radiance into my being. I have even gone so far as to pull up a massive number of Google photos taken by fellow leaf-peepers back east, and swoon over the images. Sometimes I would get my "autumn fix" from the few brilliant persimmon trees in our area. Or if the weather turns cool and rainy, I stand by my window and get so excited that I totally do the Herman Munster thing: I raise my arms in front of me and shake my fists, smiling gleefully.

In all the time I've lived in this desert region, the season just isn't the same compared to what I hold in my nostalgic youthful memories. As a "transplant" I make do; I bake those apple crisps and pumpkin breads, I hang my harvest wreath, I arrange my decorations and flowers --- but there is wistfulness in my heart. I haven't recovered after all.

……………

Now we come to the part in this book where I provide the reader with an odd assortment of true tidbits I've collected that illuminate how weird it can be to live on this planet.

- My neighbor once went to a doctor who had food in his beard and bloodstains on his white coat.
- A friend who had dressed up as "Death" on Halloween had an aneurysm that night and nearly died. She was only in her early twenties.
- Owensboro, Kentucky has a drive-in shoe hospital.
- Kentucky has a town called Wax.
- Oregon has a town called Drain and California has a town called Weed.
- Some funny plant names are Mud Midget and Wooly Marbles.
- While a woman in our area was giving birth in the hospital, her house was being robbed.
- A man at a café told the short-order cook to make his burger well-done but to put it on a glazed donut and not on a bun. (Yes, he was joking.)
- Working as an investigator for Pinkerton, my former babysitter had to track and detain whoever was smearing poop onto the walls of a library bathroom.
- A young woman in court for a divorce proceeding started to have contractions at seven months along.
- A second grade teacher had two (unrelated) kids in her class who, although their names were not spelled like the auto parts, were called Chassie and Axel.
- One mother of five became so frazzled that she put away the iron in the freezer.
- A department store shopper won the award for one hundred percent off of everything she bought during a "secret sale," but the only thing she purchased was nylons!
- A person who was out driving drunk at 7:00 in the morning killed a jogger who was a mother of two small children.

- A friend of my daughter's who was learning to drive took a lesson from a driving instructor who told him to slow down because she was carsick!

Now, some things I would like to know are, do circus performers have incredible sex lives? They are so fit and virile – are the women performers kinky as a rule? Why do sunglasses always seem to get scratched directly in one's field of vision, and not on the side or something? Why do clothing tags have to be SO SCRATCHY? It's about time that some shirt labels are now being printed right on the clothing fabric and not on a strip that creates "tag attack." Why aren't "goomba," "ignats" and "grickle" in the dictionary? Although I don't write them, I speak them all the time!

◆◆◆◆◆◆◆◆

I love how our dog Mia likes to be in the same room as I am. Right now she's peering over the blanket she's curled against, probably wondering when I'll be ready to play again. That animal can appear so bloody angelic, the way she molds her small body up next to the pillows, reposing in perfect beauty. Sometimes I am seized with a longing to be able to capture her in paint. God made her so adorable that I can hardly stop myself from either squeezing the dickens out of her or gritting my teeth, wanting to take a bite out of her. Do you do that? There are other times though when I regret the imposition of having a dog. She is especially challenging for me in that I have to consciously monitor how much I am talking to her. Once I get to cooing, praising or questioning her, it's difficult to stop talking to myself out loud.

I embarrass myself by how easily I can mix up my words. When out walking Mia I might say, "Good jirl" instead of "Good girl" or "Good job." I have also caught myself saying that I need to "tecker for chicks" rather than "check her for ticks." I also wonder what it is that makes me fond of nicknames for my dog that begin with "B." I call her Bug, Buddy, Buster, Bumble and Buzzwink.

It figures that I would end up with a nervous dog since I'm kind of skittery, too. My mom would probably liken me to a water "skeeter" that darts around in streams. My daily walks with Mia were going just great for months, and I was attached to our sojourn together into the hills behind the house. (I nicknamed these hills "the land of the chewed-up bunnies." The local coyote crowd dines regularly on them and the neighborhood cats. Posters of missing kitties are frequently spotted in animal clinics and on phone poles.) Mia's "puppy flag" of a tail always stayed up when I told her we'd be taking a walkie. Then everything changed dramatically after we had that crazy thunderstorm. It was MOST unusual to have thunder and lightning in this state and in September as well. The nighttime sky was all blinky-blinky! After that storm, Mia was a nervous wreck for nearly six months before her enthusiasm returned for walking in the neighborhood.

◆◆◆◆◆◆◆◆

The following section features several poems
inspired by my trips along the seaside and up into the hills.

Tongue twister derived from slogging
through hillside sand:
TRUDGING DRUDGERY

Another tongue twister:
PREPOSTEROUS PROSPERITY
(OR preposterous posterity)

Faux Poetry - A collection dedicated to the beauty around me

After a plummeting rainfall, I took a walk by the bay with our dog Mia. The water had the most mesmerizing calm to it that I had ever seen. A frog croaked. Twenty murres floated by. A lone duck hunter floated past too. The sky and bay were both four shades of blue and deep grey. In two places I noticed a gleaming pale purple on the surface of the water.

My walks here at the inlet are religious. It is always in this place that I feel a part me splits off as soon as I arrive, where an aspect of myself leaves to fly side by side with the angels. Stepping through the small eucalyptus grove onto the shore, I witness the daily miracle of wildlife at peace (when it's not hunting season). The flocks, gaggles and pods of various creatures unite for their early morning feast. These beings are making music and my soul silently joins in their chorus. I am profoundly uplifted by the simple notes of their burbling, and by the hue of blue currents moving around me. This humble bird sanctuary gives my soul sanctuary.

The streaks of light were sketched into the grey strips of clouds and spread across the carpeted canyon valley, blue strokes intermingling. I spied an opening in the clouds that was shaped like a heart. There was no need to scan the trail for rattlesnakes on this rain-pending day. Walking below the overhang of sheltering manzanita limbs gave me a protected feeling. The extended archway of the branches produced not one stretch of spiderspin across my face.

The wind blows loudly in my ears
yet it fills my being with silence.

It shifts me into the present.

I am a perfect part of the scenery –
the dunes, the laurel and paintbrush, the clouds and white caps -
we are calm and quiet together.

There's something so perfect about starting out on a walk and seeing a tiny hummingbird perched calmly on a bare tree branch. It is God's artwork, a living haiku.

I like how the California everlasting plant tucks itself away off the path, hiding in between the bushes and keeping its gift close to itself (it has a wonderfully unique fragrance). Growing up I felt like that. I saw a small gem in me, but I preferred keeping it safe and out of regular view.

I love it when the sky that's cooking up a storm looks so 3-D. There's the blue backdrop, then the layer of puffy grey and white clouds, then another layer of foamy white streaks spread here and there. Shapes float past, a slow parade above me.

The coming of the first rain brought a fresh look to my patch of sky, as if a brand new gallery of marvelous paintings had just opened in town.

With rain in the forecast the clouds over the soccer field looked like smoky white Cheetos™ laced together, all arranged very evenly. The hills had a thin ribbony whipped cream cloud layer that covered the visible expanse of their range for miles. Undisturbed tracks of quail, lizard and beetle in the sand looked identical to the crisscross pattern of the ticking on a baseball. These creatures had been busy at dawn like the snails that ransacked our strawberries. Quail cast out their morning calls to each other that sounded like a honking version of the game "telephone."

It doesn't seem to be purely coincidence that the blue lupine and the yellow bush monkey flower grace the trail side by side in lovely color harmony. One could surmise that God planted them that way on purpose. Should that be true, then surely He is involved in our tiny mundane lives.

Loosely threaded cloud puffs
formed a matted coverlet to the east,
moving onward to cool down the neighboring towns.
On the west side of sky the blues varied in tone,
just like a paint chip sample
with its shades intensifying at each level.

The shifting sun cast golden tones onto the shiny eucalyptus skin, while the charcoal-smudged cotton ball of a cloud gave the bark a dull grey. Flower heads were slumped forward after the storm. Intermittent sun-glow brought forth a heat that allowed the nasturtiums to release their cucumbery scent. I had just given myself an inexpensive aromatherapy session.

I stopped to really listen to the foghorn and allow its soothing rhythm to penetrate me, scattering my daily concerns away. It blew my cares off of me so that I felt cleansed, the same way a cold mist can chill and refresh you on the outside but your fleece jacket keeps you toasty warm on the inside.

Eight pelicans that were cruising in a straight formation appeared to be on an invisible roller coaster moving gently over several small hills. Three dogs chasing each other systematically on the cliff reminded me of those tiny trains that run endlessly around their track inside a snow dome.

Strolling by the bay I observe beauty everywhere my head turns. In every direction a lovely image greets me: the baby wake from a small paddling coot, the gentle sway of the pampas grass, the shimmery backs of the overturned kayaks in the bright sun and the deep hue of blue in the ripples. It all gives me a balanced feeling and the happy anticipation of floating away.

God I thank you
for Your blue
It means so much to me
to see

179

High tide brings me a feeling of warm satisfaction. I like knowing that the paths that wind around the estuary are submerged but always there – in the way that Spirit and possibility are always there, just beneath the surface.

As the fog lifts at the bay I see art in motion. The canvas changes moment by moment as new shapes are revealed. More of the dunes become exposed. More of the veiled waterfront property is visible. The light brings forth deeper reflections on the water. At low tide the inlet is a completely different setting. A new stream has replaced the swelling tide. All mossy earthen colors have painted the scene over.

The silence of the snoozing otter gives contrast to the cacophony of the screeching gulls hovering around Morro Rock. The greeting of the blue heron on its early morning flight across the channel has a similar squawk to that of a baby pterodactyl from a kid's dinosaur cartoon. Hearing the brief "spitty" exhale of the harbor seal reminds me that the rhythmic lapping of the small waves upon the shore is like the constant in-and-out breath of the universe.

Thank you God for the marvelous diversity of Your creation. Seeing the seals do their water ballet side-by-side brings me such gratitude for these simple gifts. To be honest, though, I don't admire Your having fashioned the potato bug, cockroach or mosquito.

I could hear the sea at home but I needed to get physically closer to it.
Down near the shore I had a brief "I am that" moment –
I could see the setting as a perfect picture;
how my sitting and watching on the back of a skiff

made it complete.

The scene cried out to be admired.

I am that puffy mist crawling over the mudflats.
I am that band of shadow moving back and forth,
the clouds painting shade across the bright eelgrass.
I am that puddle and that long log of aged driftwood,

and That.

In Praise of Spring

Cold sun and chilly whipped air
The purply pink flowers are splotchy dollops on the ground
More dog walkers appear on the muddy trail
Strong wind hushes the birds.

Last night's shower still sparkles
Sage and poison oak growing side by side
(the good ole' yin-yang in everything)
The scents of all mountain things growing fill me with nourishment.

Below this hilltop the dark ocean curls and cascades
It was an Island of the Blue Dolphins moment
Me alone on a cliff, grounded in the earth
and in my womanly strength;
connected to the powerful Ocean Mother below me.

Living here we are as lucky as Grecians.

Welcome Spring

I am lulled into tranquility by the heating pad of the sun
by the welcome sounds of the bluejay squawk
the flapping of the doggie door
the soft tinkle of the chimes as the breeze ripples past.
The breath of heaven waves its tufty pink clumps at me as if in
acknowledgement of my admiration.

The pleasant world on this fine spring day bids me welcome
I breathe it in with the utmost gratitude
I call my greetings to the rose bushes as they stretch out, breaking
through the crust of their winter pruning.

The neighbor's cat perches calmly on the fence between our houses,
ignoring our dog's shouts, waiting patiently to claim its sunning spot on
our trampoline.

Now the barking has ceased but the cat knows she is not yet welcome
here. Yard patrol is on duty, nose to the ground.

Soon the flowers on the hillside will be dazzling us
parading for us in their bright new frocks of color, complete with zesty
perfume.
For now I'm content to see them in my mind's eye, shining with vitality.
I patiently wait to claim their beauty
I wait as they build from the moist soil their limbs and raiments --
when finished, proclaiming, "We welcome you two-footed creatures to
the majesty of our springtime unfolding."

Garden Reverie

In an ideal world
I wouldn't drink coffee
I'd do yoga regularly
my dog would obey my every command
and humans wouldn't be warlike

But today
this tasty cup of coffee begs me to sit down for a moment
in the shade, rocking on the patio swing
and take time to observe the forms around me
in their simple quietness

The bright ripe strawberries I picked couldn't look more perfect
the dangling pole beans hang in total surrender – their job is done
our late tomatoes are aglow in burgeoning color

Newly opened rosebuds transfix me with their grace, and I admire how
dazzling they would be in a watercolor
if I could paint

But right now I'm just happy to look
To be still

And wonder

Island Introspection

Our lives are a little like sea glass
For a time our solid forms hold that which we think is our purpose
We buy into the illusion that we are in shiny separate containers
Our usefulness seems brief and then
we are tossed out
If lucky, broken
Where the shininess that was really inside
still fills us

Our sharp edges are whittled down
Lovingly smoothed over by the waves of time
We become gentle, transparent
Simple beautiful tokens that reflect the mystery of our individual
metamorphoses

How soft we are
When we yield to that vast ocean of love

I want nothing more
than to feel the sun and breeze on my skin
and to gaze upon the garden of colors before me

The twittering finches add to the perfection of the moment

God has composed for me a spring sonnet
complete with cheeps, ocean murmur and the laughter of my child
Their notes flow into me
my soul's contentment contributing to the chorus

Heard only by me
on this glorious spring day
this afternoon of thankfulness

I need nothing else to be complete

Final Thoughts

Writing is gardening with words. They both dig up the dirt. In putting this book together I found that I was raking, weeding, composting, pruning and sowing. I did the other kind of sewing as well-- threading, hemming up the length and patching. With my pen at the ready I can hardly wait to start again.

****

Waking in the middle of the night
I arose two seconds before I heard an owl hooting
and it gave me a gentle reminder of how much I love God's
creations
and how wondrous it is to hear their voices

I am especially enamored of the mockingbird and its vast trove
of sounds

If death were to capture me tomorrow
I would feel better knowing that I left behind
      some seedlings growing
      a family and dog that loved me
      and my whimsical notions written down.

****

I hope my little book has given you some inspiration to keep a notebook---not only is it fun, but forgiveness and self-love come more easily when, page after page, you can clearly see the paths you have taken to wholeness through writing.